Manufacturing Tail Risk: A Perspective on the Financial Crisis of 2007–2009

Manufacturing Tail Risk: A Perspective on the Financial Crisis of 2007–2009

Viral V. Acharya

New York University
New York, NY 10012, USA
vacharya@stern.nyu.edu

Thomas Cooley

New York University
New York, NY 10012, USA

Matthew Richardson

New York University
New York, NY 10012, USA

Ingo Walter

New York University
New York, NY 10012, USA

now
the essence of knowledge

Boston – Delft

Foundations and Trends® in Finance

Published, sold and distributed by:
now Publishers Inc.
PO Box 1024
Hanover, MA 02339
USA
Tel. +1-781-985-4510
www.nowpublishers.com
sales@nowpublishers.com

Outside North America:
now Publishers Inc.
PO Box 179
2600 AD Delft
The Netherlands
Tel. +31-6-51115274

The preferred citation for this publication is V. V. Acharya, T. Cooley, M. Richardson and I. Walter, Manufacturing Tail Risk: A Perspective on the Financial Crisis of 2007–2009, Foundations and Trends® in Finance, vol 4, no 4, pp 247–325, 2009

ISBN: 978-1-60198-340-4

Foundations and Trends® in Finance
Volume 4 Issue 4, 2009

Editorial Scope

Foundations and Trends® in Finance will publish survey and tutorial articles in the following topics:

- Corporate Governance
- Corporate Financing
- Dividend Policy and Capital Structure
- Corporate Control
- Investment Policy
- Agency Theory and Information
- Market Microstructure
- Portfolio Theory
- Financial Intermediation
- Investment Banking
- Market Efficiency
- Security Issuance
- Anomalies and Behavioral Finance
- Asset-Pricing Theory
- Asset-Pricing Models
- Tax Effects
- Liquidity
- Equity Risk Premium
- Pricing Models and Volatility
- Fixed Income Securities
- Computational Finance
- Futures Markets and Hedging
- Financial Engineering
- Interest Rate Derivatives
- Credit Derivatives
- Financial Econometrics
- Estimating Volatilities and Correlations

Information for Librarians

Foundations and Trends® in Finance, 2009, Volume 4, 4 issues. ISSN paper version 1567-2395. ISSN online version 1567-2409. Also available as a combined paper and online subscription.

Foundations and Trends® in
Finance
Vol. 4, No. 4 (2009) 247–325

DOI: 10.1561/0500000025

now
the essence of knowledge

Manufacturing Tail Risk: A Perspective on the Financial Crisis of 2007–2009

Viral V. Acharya[1], Thomas Cooley[2], Matthew Richardson[3] and Ingo Walter[4]

[1] *Stern School of Business, New York University, New York, NY 10012, USA, vacharya@stern.nyu.edu*
[2] *Stern School of Business, New York University, New York, NY 10012, USA*
[3] *Stern School of Business, New York University, New York, NY 10012, USA*
[4] *Stern School of Business, New York University, New York, NY 10012, USA*

Abstract

We argue that the fundamental cause of the financial crisis of 2007–2009 was that large, complex financial institutions ("LCFIs") took excessive leverage in the form of manufacturing tail risks that were systemic in nature and inadequately capitalized. We employ a set of headline facts about the build-up of such risk exposures to explain how and why LCFIs adopted this new banking model during 2003–2Q 2007, relative to earlier models. We compare the crisis with other episodes in the United States, in particular, the panic of 1907, the failure of Continental Illinois and the Savings and Loan crisis. We conclude that several principal imperfections, in particular, distortions induced by regulation and government guarantees, developed in decades preceding the current one, allowing LCFIs to take on excessive systemic risk. We also examine alternative explanations for the financial crisis. We conclude that while moral hazard problems in the originate-and-distribute model of banking, excess liquidity due to global imbalances and mispricing of risk due to behavioral biases have some merit as candidates, they fail to explain the complete spectrum of evidence on the crisis.

Contents

1 Introduction **1**

2 How Did We Get There? **5**

2.1 The Panic of 1907 and Its Aftermath 5
2.2 Bank Competition, Financial Innovation and Risk-Taking in the Last Decades of the 20th Century 10
2.3 Risk-Taking Incentives of Financial Institutions 16

3 The New Banking Model of Manufacturing Tail Risk **25**

4 Alternative Explanations of the Financial Crisis **45**

5 Conclusion **65**

A Appendix: Tail Risk in the Rest of the World **69**

References **75**

1

Introduction

There is virtually universal agreement that the fundamental cause of the global economic and financial crisis of 2007–2009 was the combination of a credit boom and a housing bubble. In the five-year period covering 2002–2007, the ratio of debt to national income in the United States increased from 3.75:1 to 4.75:1. It had taken the whole preceding decade to produce an increase in aggregate debt of this magnitude. Moreover, from 2002 to 2007, house prices grew at an unprecedented rate of 11% per year. Why? With the benefit of hindsight, an extraordinary flood of liquidity and accommodative monetary policy that ignored asset prices produced extraordinarily low expected real interest rates. This appeared to have left investors scrambling for "alpha" — the so-called "search for yield" — that encouraged all kinds of borrowers to use maximum leverage. Households, corporations, financial firms, investors, and even countries borrowed heavily. When the "bubble" burst, a severe economic crisis was bound to come. At the household level, families whose homes were highly leveraged and whose equity represented 35% of their wealth would not be able to consume as they did through 2007. The real economy was bound to feel the brunt of the inevitable correction

It is much less clear, however, why this combination of events led to such a severe financial crisis — why we had such widespread and sometimes catastrophic failures of financial institutions along with the freezing-up of capital markets. The systemic crisis that ensued reduced the supply of capital to creditworthy institutions and individuals, resulted in a sudden sharp decline in global trade and production, and amplified the effects on the real economy worldwide

We argue that what made this economic shock unique, and led to such a severe financial crisis was the behavior of many of the large, complex financial institutions (LCFIs) — the universal banks and financial conglomerates, investment banks, insurance companies, and (in rare cases) even hedge funds — that today dominate the financial industry. These LCFIs ignored their own business model of securitization and chose *not* to transfer credit risk to other investors. Instead, they employed securitization to manufacture and retain tail risk that was systemic in nature and inadequately capitalized. Institutions matter, and in this case the robustness of the financial architecture built over two decades or so showed severe weaknesses

The legitimate and valuable purpose of securitization is to spread risk. It does so by removing large concentrations of risk from the balance sheets of financial institutions, and placing small concentrations into the hands of a large number of investors who get paid an acceptable price for bearing that risk. But especially from 2003 to 2007, the main purpose of securitization appeared not to have been to share risks with investors, but to make an end-run around capital-adequacy regulations applied to financial intermediaries. The net result was to keep the risk concentrated in the financial institutions themselves — and, indeed, to keep that risk at a greatly magnified level because of the overleveraging that it allowed. When the risk actually materialized — the housing bubble burst — these institutions experienced wholesale failures, resulting in the greatest systemic crisis we have seen since the Great Depression.

Our assessment can be restated in a different way. It is now well recognized that given limited liability, levered firms have incentives to shift the profile of their assets toward higher risk (the so-called "risk-shifting" argument of Jensen and Meckling, 1976). Left to market devices, agency costs arising due to these incentives should be priced by creditors. In turn, the firms should have incentives to limit agency costs *ex ante*. In this view, all outcomes are assumed to be second best in equilibrium. However, this view needs to be refined for financial firms, since they have an important set of creditors — the government and the taxpayer — as a consequence of implicit and explicit subsidies. Government guarantees are often not priced fully (or at all). This distorts financial firms' cost of capital and their capital budgeting, inducing a preference for higher risk and higher leverage. Recognizing this moral hazard problem, regulation such as capital requirements are put in place.

As a result, the objective function of financial firms can be viewed as maximizing shareholder value given the mispricing of agency costs in government guarantees and subject to capital-adequacy requirements. While these firms can maximize their objective functions by enhancing overall value, that is, taking positive net present value investments, they can also circumvent capital requirements if regulation is lax and the resulting "regulatory arbitrage" is opaque and complex enough that markets cannot fully price the resulting agency costs. Viewed in this perspective, LCFI behavior during 2003–2007 clearly shows profit maximization by extensively exploiting gaps in the regulatory constraint rather than by undertaking positive net present value investments. The end result was the classic excessive leverage build-up in the financial sector. But since the manner in which such gaps were exploited was complex and opaque, the crisis that resulted was not well-anticipated by markets and led to severe spillovers to both financial and real sectors of the economy.

Section 2 of this monograph begins with a brief history of how the U.S. financial system evolved into its current form. We pay special attention to the risk-taking incentives of financial institutions and the breakdown of the regulatory system-wide protections that had emanated from the experience of the Great Depression.

Section 3 proposes a set of headline facts about the precise manner in which banks built tail (systemic) risk exposures during 2003–2Q 2007 in large measure to get around capital requirements, in contrast to their earlier business models. We explain how lax regulation contributed to these outcomes, especially during the 2003–2005 period.

In light of these headline facts, Section 4 examines alternative explanations for the financial crisis: (1) Failure of the originate-and-distribute model, and the role played by rating agencie; (2) Panics in response to efficient securitization undertaken by the financial sector; (3) Global imbalances; (4) "Animal spirits" and mispricing of risks; (5) Loose monetary policy, especially in the United States; and, (6) Illiquidity-induced crisis (rather than an insolvency-induced one). By and large, we conclude that global imbalances and loose monetary policy were relevant proximate contributors to the crisis by producing an asset-price bubble in the United States that ultimately led to the large negative economic shock; concomitantly, the contemporaneous business model of LCFIs to concentrate tail risks on their balance sheets rather than distribute them translated the economic shock into a full-blown crisis in the financial sector which was soon transferred to the real sector. We explain why none of the other alternative explanations does much to help explain the complete spectrum of available evidence on risks undertaken by banks.

Section 5 provides concluding remarks and a brief discussion of possible remedies to charge banks for manufacturing tail risks and to contain such propensity in the first place. Though we focus on the United States for most of our discussion, we also discuss risk-taking and realized losses by LCFIs in other parts of the world. This latter discussion is contained in Section 4, where we consider the role of global imbalances, and in a separate Appendix.

2

How Did We Get There?

Financial crises have many common features. Preceding any crisis, there is almost invariably some sort of asset price bubble, a corresponding credit boom, and large capital inflows into the economy (see, for example, Reinhart and Rogoff (2008)). This is not too surprising. A financial crisis by definition involves a precipitous drop in nominal wealth and an increase in volatility, which widen credit spreads. That said, it remains likely that, while these characteristics are necessary, they are not sufficient to define a true financial crisis. Its severity fundamentally depends on the underlying financial sector's exposure to such conditions together with the overall market's uncertainty about the financial sector's exposure to the developments at hand.

This section maps out how the U.S. financial system got to the point at which the crisis of 2007–2009 emerged. We begin a century earlier, with the panic of 1907.

2.1 The Panic of 1907 and Its Aftermath

The panic of 1907 was triggered in the curbside "shadow" stock market that was organized outside the New York Stock Exchange (NYSE).[1]

[1] The best recent account of the Panic of 1907 is Bruner and Carr (2007).

Many companies were traded literally on the street curb in a vibrant market that eventually became the American Stock Exchange. Why? Because the market was more efficient and more accessible than the NYSE at the time. In October of 1907, two brothers, Augustus and Otto Heinze, tried to corner the market in United Copper Company stock by executing a short squeeze. Their scheme failed, and the price of United Copper plummeted. The Heinze brothers who had hatched the scheme turned out to have been heavily involved with a number of banks and brokerages. When their curb market scheme collapsed, it quickly raised concerns about the safety of the banks that had lent the money to back their scheme. Within days a state bank in Montana owned by Augustus Heinze failed. Augustus was also President of the Mercantile National Bank of New York at the time, and was forced to resign because of his association with the corner and the failed Montana Bank. News of his resignation immediately created a panic that caused a run on the Mercantile Bank.

The panic spread and led to pressure on other banks' stocks and deposits in those banks — a classic case of contagion. Noteworthy was the Knickerbocker Trust Co., the third largest trust bank in New York, whose President Charles Barney was suspected of having helped to finance the Heinze scheme. The run on the Knickerbocker Trust Co. forced it to close its doors and suspend operations. Charles Barney committed suicide not long after. The panic continued to spread to other trust companies and, within days, a large number of banks had failed.

The problem that faced banks — and financial markets more broadly at the time — was the contradiction inherent in fractional reserve banking. All such institutions were engaged in intermediation of one form or another with less than 100% reserves. When depositors became concerned and demanded their money back, even solvent financial institutions could find their cash and gold reserves insufficient to meet demands for cash and were forced to shut their doors. The institutions that had evolved (see Gorton, 1985) to address the problem of temporary liquidity shortages were bank clearing house associations that pooled resources to provide liquidity to individual members in times of stress and perform many of the functions of a central bank. But two problems emerged in this arrangement during the Panic of 1907. The first was that a private clearing house association can itself face the risk of default. The second was that trust companies in New York were excluded from membership in the banks' Clearing House Association.

Some calm was restored during the 1907 panic by the intervention of J. P. Morgan, who assumed a central role in trying to prevent it from spreading. Morgan had examined the books of the Knickerbocker Trust and concluded it was insolvent and had to be closed. When the panic spread to the Trust Company of America it too turned to Morgan for help. He and his associates concluded that the bank was indeed solvent, but would need a great deal of liquidity to survive. Morgan met with other bankers, the Secretary of the Treasury and John D. Rockefeller, and convinced them to work together to stop the panic.

The joint effort turned out to be successful in the short run. Morgan had temporarily saved the day, but that was not the end of his intervention. Short-term loans were unavailable. Call money rates soared to 60% and more, and no loans took place. The troubles of the banks spread to the stock exchange, which lost 48% of its value in a matter of weeks. Many prominent brokerages were threatened with collapse. New York City was on the verge of bankruptcy. And, within a short time the Trust Companies themselves were again on the verge of collapse. J.P. Morgan invited the most prominent banking and trust company leaders to a meeting at his home and, famously, locked them in the library until they agreed to a plan to help the weakest of their members through the crisis.

There were many lessons to be learned from the Panic of 1907, most notably concerning liquidity and capital, which would play out over the next quarter century and remained trenchant a hundred years later. On the liquidity front, it became accepted that there needed to be a credible lender of last resort who can restore trust in the system and its institutions. And on the capital front, it was realized that since information regarding solvency of financial institutions is difficult to gather and incredibly valuable, if there is no institution to provide it, the risk of bank runs is high.

Essentially starting with the Panic of 1907 and carrying through the banking crisis of August 1914, the stock market crash of 1929, and the banking panics of 1930, 1931, and early 1933, what emerged was a complete overhaul of the U.S. financial system. While the Federal Reserve — and its role as the lender of last resort — was created in 1913, the majority of the changes were enacted in 1933 and 1934.[2] These regulatory initiatives were enacted precisely because policymakers recognized that the severity of the banking crisis and the ensuing period, commonly referred to as the Great Depression, were inexorably inter-related.

Specifically, the 1929 stock market crash, the collapse of production and wealth that followed, and the continued volatility of financial markets in the 1930s, led consumers and businesses to dramatically reduce spending, caused extraordinarily high bankruptcy rates among businesses, and brought about the disappearance by failure or acquisition of nearly half of all American financial institutions, often involving classis bank runs triggered by suspected insolvency. These came in the form of three separate waves of banking panics during 1930–1933. The economic forces that created and perpetuated the Great Depression have been much discussed and debated, and we will simply note here a general consensus that the contractionary monetary policies that the Federal Reserve Board pursued at the time were a contributory factor in the banking crises and their real-sector consequences (Friedman and Schwartz, 1971). Prices of goods and services fell approximately 25% between 1929 and 1933. This in turn led to debt deflation, a phenomenon by which the collateral underlying loans shrinks in value, causing the real burden of debt to rise, leading the economy to spiral further downward (Bernanke, 2000).

Policymakers at the time recognized that, even with the liquidity backstop by the government, the problem with the U.S. financial system was that uncertainty about insolvency (i.e., bank capital) could cause a run on the system. The Banking Act of the 1933 solved the uncertainty problem that led to bank runs by providing deposit insurance through the creation of the Federal Deposit Insurance Corporation (FDIC). Depositors no longer had to run on the bank because the government guaranteed deposits, the bulk of bank liabilities. Along with

[2] Friedman and Schwartz (1971) and Meltzer (2004).

this government backstop came the fact that deposit insurance creates moral hazard — the incentive for banks to undertake greater risk than they would otherwise have taken without deposit insurance. Regulators and policymakers understood that deposit insurance could lead to excessive risk-taking, so they set up a number of counteracting barriers.

In particular, banks would have to pay fees to be part of the deposit insurance system. So, at least, on an *ex ante* basis, regulators took into account the cost of the insurance. Deposit insurance was limited in magnitude per account, thus restricting the size of the banks. Most important, there were the so-called Glass-Steagall restrictions: the risk-taking activities of banks were ring-fenced to the extent there was a separation of commercial banking (taking deposits and making commercial loans) from arguably more risky investment banking activities (underwriting and dealing in corporate debt, equity securities, and municipal revenue bonds). In addition, there would be enhanced supervision of individual banks, generally in the form of minimum capital requirements, as well as winding-down provisions in the case of failure. Capital requirements represent protection against the risk-shifting incentive arising from deposit insurance, because the incentive only exists when leverage and/or asset volatility are high.

While there are many reasons for the relative calm of the U.S. financial system for the fifty years after the Great Depression, many analysts point to the financial regulation that was enacted in 1933, complemented by securities and investment legislation enacted in 1933, 1934, and 1940.

But starting in the early 1980s, the U.S. banking system began to show some cracks. Ignoring international shocks such as the emerging market crisis of 1981, the real estate crises in Japan and the Nordic countries in 1991, the Mexican "tequila" crisis of 1994, and the Asian contagion of 1997, it may be surprising to recall that the United States suffered a number of events during this time that could have led to financial crises that might have been far more serious than they turned out to be — the failure of Continental Illinois in 1984, the S&L crisis of the 1980s, the stock market crash of 1987, the LTCM crisis in the fall of 1998, and the burst of the dotcom bubble in 2000. So what happened during this period that ultimately made the serenity of the

U.S. financial system fade away and ultimately evaporate in the most recent crisis?

2.2 Bank Competition, Financial Innovation and Risk-Taking in the Last Decades of the 20th Century

There is considerable debate about why the banking system changed so much in the 1980s, but the general consensus is that technology changed the nature of banking and therefore competition in the banking sector (Kroszner, 2000; Kroszner and Strahan, 2007). Some of these technological changes included (i) the development of the automated teller machine (ATM) that reduced geographical ties between banks and depositors, (ii) the proliferation of money market funds and cash management accounts outside the banking system, and (iii) the increase in the types of communication channels, reducing again the ties between local bankers and depositors. In other words, traditional lines of business of banks no longer enjoyed their privileged status as financial intermediaries.

In an important paper, Keeley (1990) uses the increase in bank competition as an explanation for the Savings and Loan (S&L) crisis of the 1980s. Prior to the aforementioned changes in financial technology, banks and thrifts enjoyed monopolistic advantages and their charters had significant franchise value. But once this franchise value was diminished, the benefits associated with risk-shifting and exploiting the guarantees of deposit insurance increased. In general, there is convincing evidence of risk-shifting related to deregulation and increased banking competition that was a prime explanation for the S&L crisis (Saunders et al., 1990; Cordell et al., 1993; Kroszner and Strahan, 1996; Hovakimian and Kane, 2000).

Around the same time, the institutional side of banking also changed dramatically. For example, there was tremendous growth in the so-called "shadow" banking system, i.e., financial institutions outside the traditional banking system that provide very similar services (Adrian and Shin, 2009; Acharya et al., 2009a; Gorton, 2009). The shadow banking system includes derivatives — futures, options, swaps — as well as repos and money market funds, securitization of loans in the mortgage, corporate, and household sectors, and an increasing importance of public equity and bond markets. As an illustration, the amount of assets of the financial sector held by depository institutions dropped from 60% in 1950 to less than 30% in 2006 (Kroszner and Melick, 2009). In Section 3 we provide a detailed analysis of this banking model that took hold in the 1980s and appeared to flourish thereafter.

Partly because of these dramatic changes in the nature of financial intermediation, there was general recognition that certain provisions of the Banking Act of 1933 — those most commonly referred to as the Glass-Steagall provisions — had become obsolete. This process of erosion of the allowable scope of commercial bank activities started in the mid 1980s with the reinterpretation of Section 20 subsidiaries of banks (which were permitted to carry out Glass-Steagall prohibited activities within certain limits), later with the Riegel-Neal Interstate Banking and Branching Efficiency Act of 1994, and then finally with the formal repeal of Glass-Steagall through the Gramm-Leach-Bliley Financial Services Modernization Act of 1999. The deregulatory environment continued thereafter, with the Commodity Futures Modernization Act of 2000, and in August 2004 with the amendment to the "net capital rule" of the Securities Exchange Act of 1934 allowing investment banks to dramatically increase leverage and put them on equal footing with universal banks under Basel II.

The result of these changes was to leave the financial system for the most part unprotected by the safety infrastructure that had been created in the 1930s, and, in many ways, even weaker in a regulatory sense than at any time since the early 1900s. This is not to argue that the Banking Act of the 1930s should necessarily have remained in place, only that whatever replaced them should have been mindful of the market failures that led to their passage in the first place. One only has to look at two episodes in the 1980s to understand this point.

2.2.1 Continental Illinois[3]

In 1982, federal regulators decided to close the Oklahoma-based Penn Square Bank, a $436-million asset bank that specialized in oil and

[3] This account relies heavily on FDIC (1997).

gas sector loans. Penn Square originated large volumes of loans to the historically risky exploration sector of the U.S. energy industry, which began to suffer as energy prices fell after 1981. The seventh largest bank in the United States, Continental Illinois, had invested aggressively alongside or through Penn Square and held hundreds of millions of dollars of Penn Square's book of loans. Continental had made many other loans to the energy sector and had also expanded its business risk by lending large amounts to developing countries to help them finance external debt incurred in the energy crises of the 1970s. In 1982, Mexico was forced to begin renegotiating its syndicated bank debt, triggering the emerging market debt crisis that was not fully resolved for almost a decade.

While many other U.S. commercial banks followed the same strategy of lending to credit hungry markets in the late 1970s, Continental's credit exposures were compounded by a funding strategy that was unusual at the time. Traditionally, banks fund growth in their lending activities by attracting larger volumes of savings from retail depositors. Continental, however, had a limited retail presence, due in part to federal and local banking regulations. The bank depended heavily on funding from the wholesale money markets. Indeed, by 1981, Continental gained most of its funding through federal funds and by selling short-term certificates of deposit on the wholesale money markets. Only 20% of its funding came from traditional retail deposits.

Continental had pursued an aggressive growth strategy and assumed concentrated risk financed mostly with short-term wholesale debt. When the energy sector turned sour and the developing countries renegotiated their debt, Continental was unusually vulnerable to the views of the wholesale funding markets. In 1984, investors and creditors lost confidence and in a precursor to the crisis of 2007–2008, Continental was quickly shut out of its usual sources of funding in the domestic and Eurodollar interbank markets. In May of 1984, Continental experienced what the FDIC described as a high-speed electronic bank run. To stem the panic, regulatory agencies and the banking industry arranged massive emergency funding for the bank. The fear was that a failure of Continental would undermine the entire banking system. As a matter of fact, more than 2,300 banks had correspondent accounts with Continental.

In an extremely controversial decision, the Federal Deposit Insurance Corporation tried to stop the bank run by extending a guarantee to uninsured depositors and creditors at the bank. This was arguably the beginning of the notion that some banks should be considered "too big to fail". The emergency help was followed by a package of permanent measures, making Continental the largest bank in the history of U.S. banking ever to be rescued by government agencies. Unable to find a takeover partner, the FDIC ended up owning more than 80% of Continental. Management was fired, the board replaced and the bank was returned to the private sector in an IPO, later to be sold at a significant premium to Bank of America. The FDIC's share of the bill to rescue the bank was later calculated to be $1.1 billion. Although many considered the rescue of Continental under the leadership of Fed Chairman Paul A. Volcker a crisis management *tour de force*, it nevertheless signaled to unsecured creditors that they were likely to be fully protected against losses by the government under systemic risk circumstances. Market discipline was not eroded in the case of shareholders, who were wiped out, but it was eroded in the case of creditors, thereby creating moral hazard for the future.

The Continental story provides a classic example of how a sharp drop in confidence can lead counterparties in the wholesale markets to suddenly withdraw funding from a damaged bank, spinning the institution into a funding liquidity crisis as potentially fatal as any nineteenth-century run on a bank by retail depositors. It should have been a warning call that systemic risk can build up quickly in a credit expansion cycle — outside of the traditional banking technology (deposits) — and needs to be priced and regulated accordingly. Continental Illinois should have been the canary in the coal mine. It showed that the regulatory system crafted in the 1930s needed serious updating. Instead, the problem was soon forgotten and eventually resurfaced with a vengeance.

2.2.2 The Savings and Loan Crisis

The most serious post-war crisis in the United States banking sector was the Savings and Loan (S&L) Crisis of the late 1980s. It is often blamed (with at least some justification) on the more permissive regulatory environment that evolved during the Reagan Administration (White, 1991), and was repeated during the Clinton Administration a decade later. That is not the entire story, however, and it is an episode that contains valuable lessons for the crisis of 2007–2009.

U.S. Savings and Loan institutions, as distinct from commercial banks, were also a product of the Great Depression. They were created to serve the public policy goal of encouraging home ownership. The Federal Home Loan Bank Act of 1932 created the Federal Home Loan Bank System to provide liquidity and low-cost financing for S&Ls. There were twelve regional Home Loan Banks that were owned by their members and were under the supervision of the Federal Home Loan Bank Board (FHLBB). The National Housing Act of 1934 created the Federal Savings and Loan Insurance Corporation (FSLIC) to provide deposit insurance for S&Ls similar to what the FDIC provided for commercial banks. In contrast to the FDIC, which was established as an independent agency, the FSLIC was placed under the authority of the FHLBB.

For decades, the FHLBB's examination, supervision, and regulation capabilities were relatively poorly developed, in part because S&Ls had a narrowly defined role in the intermediation sector and not much scope for expanding it. S&Ls took in household savings, on which they paid relatively low interest rates, and lent at attractive interest rates on thirty year fixed rate mortgages. This model began to change with the high inflation of the 1970s when interest rates soared in response to accelerating inflation during the Carter Administration. Deposits began to flee the S&Ls in pursuit of higher returns and, even when Congress lifted caps on deposit interest rates, the S&Ls were still being squeezed on the other end by their portfolios of 30-year fixed rate mortgages. They needed to find other sources of income. As described earlier, many economists view this as the period when S&Ls moved more toward a risk-shifting model, exploiting their federal deposit insurance backstop. To accomplish this, the S&Ls needed to circumnavigate or erode existing regulations.

This began with the FHLBB itself loosening regulations covering S&Ls. It allowed the thrifts to begin issuing adjustable-rate mortgages.

Congress also encouraged S&L diversification, and explicitly authorized consumer lending and investment in commercial real estate. Both federal and state thrift regulators began relaxing restrictions on their asset allocation, relaxing safety and soundness regulation, lowering capital requirements, and changing accounting rules to make it easier for S&Ls to meet their net worth requirements. All of these changes helped the thrift industry to grow rapidly. Between 1980 and 1986, 492 new thrifts were chartered in the United States.

Things began to change when inflation was brought under control in the early 1980s by the Volcker experiment, accompanied by a serious recession. Oil prices fell to a level that made many investments in that sector unprofitable. Tax benefits for real estate investments were eliminated, and that made many projects unprofitable. Much of the financial intermediation growth between 1983 and 1985 was in commercial real estate lending. By 1985, it became clear that the thrift industry faced serious trouble. Enough S&Ls had folded or were in danger of folding that the FSLIC itself was insolvent. Efforts to recapitalize the FSLIC in 1986 and 1987 were bitterly fought by the industry, which lobbied aggressively with members of Congress. Thrift failures increased during 1987 and into 1988, but the insolvency of the FSLIC meant that rescuing troubled thrifts would cost more than the FSLIC had available in its insurance fund. As a result, the regulators could not intervene in S&Ls that had more liabilities than assets. This meant that several insolvent thrifts remained in business. These "zombies" had incentives to take even more risks in the hope that they could eventually improve their outcomes.

The crisis in the S&L industry was finally acknowledged and resolved after the inauguration of George H.W. Bush in 1989. Congress passed the Financial Institutions Reform Recovery and Enforcement Act (FIRREA) in 1989. FIRREA abolished the FHLBB and shifted regulation of S&Ls to the Office of Thrift Supervision (OTS), transferred the thrifts' deposit insurance function from the FSLIC to the FDIC, and reinstituted many of the regulatory provisions that had been weakened during the previous decade. In addition, FIRREA created the Resolution Trust Corporation (RTC) to liquidate or restructure the insolvent S&Ls.

There are several lessons from the S&L mess. The first is that when regulatory institutions have outlived their usefulness or been rendered obsolete it is not enough to just eliminate the regulatory boundaries without consideration of the risks that are being created. This was the case with the thrift industry, which had been created and developed with specific goals in mind but then morphed into something else entirely. Another lesson is that regulators can easily be captured by the industry they regulate. This was clearly the case with the FHLBB. The S&L Crisis makes it clear as well that moral hazard is an important issue. It demonstrated how critical it is to promptly close insolvent, insured financial institutions in order to minimize potential losses to the deposit insurance fund and to ensure a more efficient financial marketplace. Finally, resolution of failing financial institutions requires that any deposit insurance fund be strongly capitalized with real reserves based on meaningful risk assessments.

2.3 Risk-Taking Incentives of Financial Institutions

Given their inherently high leverage and the ease with which the risk profile of financial assets can be altered, banks, and financial institutions have incentives to take on excessive risks. Ordinarily, one would expect market mechanisms to price risks correctly and thereby ensure that risk-taking in the economy is at efficient levels. However, there are several factors — some novel and some traditional — that have ruled out such efficient outcomes.

2.3.1 The Novel Front

Financial institutions have become large and increasingly complex and opaque in their activities. This has weakened external governance that operates through capital markets (accurate prices), the market for corporate control (takeovers), and the role and functioning of boards of directors. Coincidentally there is the fact that financial risks at these institutions are now increasingly concentrated in the hands of a few "high performance" profit/risk centers. Employees (bankers, traders) engaged in these centers have skills in creating, packaging-and-repackaging, marking to market and hedging financial securities.

Since such skills are largely fungible across institutions, such employees have exerted tremendous bargaining power in their institutions and have succeeded in getting themselves rewarded through highly attractive, short-term compensation packages that provide them lucrative cash bonuses for short-run performance and what has shown itself to be effectively "fake-alpha".[4]

In the period leading up to the recent crisis, bankers were increasingly paid through short-term cash bonuses based on volume and on marked-to-market profits, rather than on the long-term profitability of their "bets".[5] So they had no incentive to discount for liquidity risk, for example, that of asset-backed securities, if their bets went wrong and nobody wanted to buy these securities. Nor was there an incentive to discount for the "maturity mismatch" inherent in special investment vehicles off the banks' balance sheets — which funded long-term assets via short-term debt (asset-backed commercial paper) that had to be rolled over frequently, generally overnight. Nor, apparently, did their managers assess the true skills of those who were generating these large "profits." In effect, regulatory arbitrage — taking on risks and financing structures that were not subject to significant capital requirements — became a primary business of the financial sector because of the short-term profits it was generating.

A case in point.[6] In the summer of 2005, UBS, the Swiss-based LCFI, became a major player in subprime mortgage collateralized debt organizations (CDOs). It purchased pools of subprime mortgages from mortgage originators and sliced and diced them so that the "super senior" tranches would receive the highest designation from

[4] Of course, whether the high level of compensation paid to bankers or traders was a symptom of weak governance or a result of the equilibrium outcome of a competitive labor market remains an open question. Gabaix and Landier (2008), for example, show how the latter mechanism can explain pay scales of such magnitude.

[5] See Rajan (2008) for an early hint of this problem with bankers' pay. Acharya et al. (2009b) and Acharya and Volpin (2010) provide models explaining why pay may have risen in the banking industry, and coincidentally risk management (governance) quality deteriorated, due to greater mobility of risk-takers across financial institutions. Acharya and Richardson (2009a, 2009b) provide a detailed account of such governance failures (see, especially, Sections 7 and 8).

[6] The following account is taken from UBS's "Shareholder Report on UBS's Write Downs," 2008, prepared for the Swiss Federal Banking Commission.

the rating agencies. The resulting AAA securities would then be sold off to investors. UBS was paid handsomely for structuring these deals. This business usually worked as intended — the credit risk that would normally be held by UBS or other banks or mortgage lenders was transferred to the better-capitalized investment community.

Starting in 2006, however, the CDO group at UBS noticed that their risk-management systems treated the AAA securities as essentially riskless, even though they yielded a premium (the proverbial free lunch). So they decided to hold onto them rather than sell them. After holding less than $5 billion of these securities in February 2006, the CDO desk was warehousing a staggering $50 billion of them by September 2007. Incredibly, this happened even though the housing market had turned south in June 2006; subprime lenders had begun to go belly-up in December 2006; and UBS itself shut down its in-house hedge fund, Dillon Read Capital Management, in May 2007 due to subprime investment losses. None of this mattered to the UBS CDO group. For every $1 of super senior securities held, it booked the premium as immediate profit. And for every dollar of current "profit" booked, the members of the CDO group received correspondingly high bonuses. The members of the group had every incentive to increase the quantity of CDOs on the balance sheet as much as possible, since their own bonuses were tied to instant profits with no recognition of any risk. In a similar fashion, by the late summer of 2007 Citigroup had accumulated over $55 billion of AAA-rated CDOs.

Many analysts have taken stories like UBS, and the fact that many of the shareholders of the failed (or near failed) institutions — Bear Stearns, Fannie Mae, Freddie Mac, Lehman Brothers, A.I.G., Merrill Lynch, Washington Mutual, Wachovia, and Citigroup — lost most of their investment in bank stocks in the crisis, as prima facie evidence of massive failure of corporate governance, i.e., between shareholders and managers. While clearly this view cannot be completely discounted, we believe it is actually secondary in importance compared to the failure of corporate governance at the debt and regulatory level. Put another way, it appears to us that shareholders of LCFIs themselves benefited from the risk-taking option inherent in such CDO bets at the expense of creditors and taxpayers.

2.3.2 The Traditional Front

To understand risk-taking incentives in large and complex financial intermediaries, we need to examine how the claim structure of the LCFIs is different from that of a regular non-financial firm. On the liability side, LCFIs are highly leveraged entities. At least 90% of the claim holders of an LCFI are debt holders (including depositors). Of course, other claimants comprise taxpayers through the numerous government guarantees in the system, most notably (i) deposit insurance, (ii) the implicit guarantee of too big to fail institutions, and (iii) the "subsidies" provided to government-sponsored enterprises like Fannie Mae and Freddie Mac. That is, the vast majority of liabilities in the U.S. financial system were the beneficiaries of some form of safety net (see, for example Marcus and Shaked, 1984; Pennacchi, 1987).

Given this structure of claims, corporate governance mechanisms that align managers with shareholders may deviate significantly from those that maximize firm value. Put differently, corporate governance mechanisms in LCFIs have to be designed so as to align the manager with the interests of the debt holders and the FDIC guarantor, as well as the shareholders. Monitoring by debt holders and the regulator are critically important components of corporate governance in LCFIs (see John and John, 1993, for details) compared to nonfinancial corporations. What kind of monitoring can one expect from debt holders? If the debt holders are depositors, deposit insurance reduces the incentives to monitor virtually to zero.

Of course, the fact that banks are covered by deposit insurance does not in itself necessarily lead to excessive risk-taking on their part. If the franchise value of their enterprise exceeds the benefits due to risk-shifting, then there might be very little effect on risk-taking as a result of deposit insurance. But two sets of consequences arose from competition that eroded the profits underlying the traditional lines of business of banks, described earlier. First, banks moved more and more into businesses focusing on noninterest income, such as trading and fee-based activities (e.g., Stiroh, 2002). Second, and more importantly, the relative value of risk-shifting increased given that value of bank charters had decreased. If the guarantees turned out to be mispriced, then the mispricing effectively removed any market discipline component of governance normally reserved for creditors. And risk-shifting within large financial intermediaries was particularly easy to do.

There is very strong evidence in the literature supporting the existence of mispriced government guarantees and the consequences arising from such guarantees. In terms of the financial crisis of 2007–2009, what was the source of regulatory failure? With respect to deposit insurance, as described earlier, there seems to be a consensus that moral hazard played an important role in both initiating and prolonging the S&L crisis. As a result, there were substantial reforms enacted to address this issue, most notably the Federal Deposit Insurance Corporation Improvement Act (FDICIA) of 1991. One of the major changes in setting FDIC premiums was to make them more risk-based. In theory, the FDIC assesses higher premiums on those institutions that pose greater risks to the insurance fund. In practice, if the deposit insurance fund was well-capitalized (i.e., 1.25% of reserves to total insured deposits), it turned out that no premiums were assessed to those banks. In fact, from 1996 to 2006, more than 90% of all banks paid very little in deposit insurance premiums.[7] Figure 2.1 effectively illustrates this point by showing a reserve ratio close to 1.25% during this period, combined with a small increase in deposit insurance fund balances.

The S&L crisis clearly suggested the need for risk-based insurance premiums to be charged to banks. The market failure was that not only was the risk-based method not applied, but no insurance premiums at all were charged to the majority of banks. This effectively meant that United States had a free deposit insurance system with little or no protection at all in place in consideration of the repeal of Glass-Steagall and the changing institutional and systemic risk exposures in the financial structure.

At first glance, the moral hazard inherent in depository institutions was limited in scope, since deposits were only a limited component of the assets (and liabilities) of the U.S. financial system. However, since the majority of assets of the financial sector were held by a small

[7] This issue was only partially addressed by the Federal Deposit Insurance Reform Act of 2005 to the extent the range of ratio of reserves to total deposits covered a wider range for which premiums would be collected.

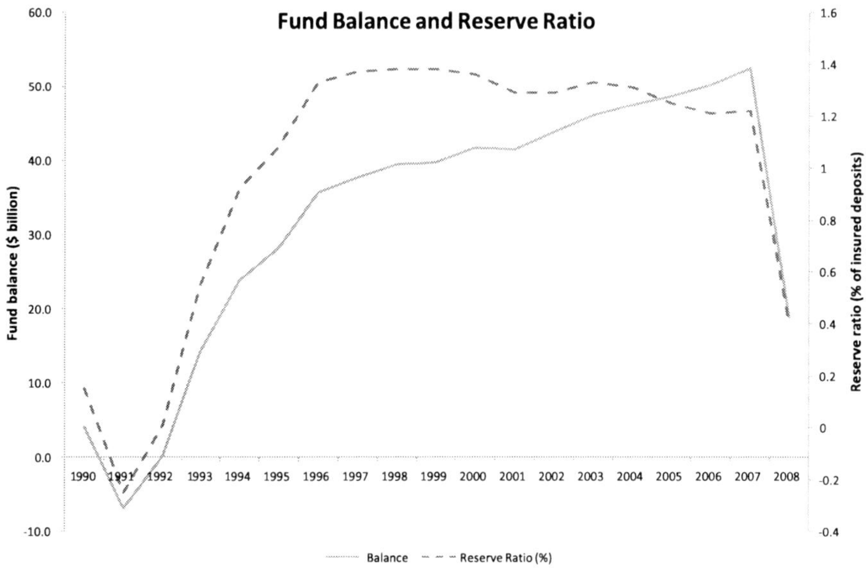

Fig. 2.1 Balances of deposit insurance fund and the reserve ratio.
Source: Federal Deposit Insurance Corporation.

number of LCFIs, the market discipline provided by debt holders was similar to that of depositors due to the too big to fail (TBTF) guarantee. Since the 1984 bailout of Continental Illinois, the issue of TBTF had been much discussed in regulatory and academic circles (see, for example Stern and Feldman, 2004; Ennis and Malek, 2005). Even before the financial crisis of 2007–2009 made the TBTF guarantee explicit, there was ample evidence that TBTF was alive and well over the previous two decades, and seriously distorted financial market pricing (see, for example O'Hara and Shaw, 1990; Penas and Unal, 2004; Morgan and Stiroh, 2005).

To understand further the importance of moral hazard and the role of government guarantees, consider the case of the government-sponsored enterprises (GSEs), Fannie Mae and Freddie Mac. Fannie Mae was founded in 1938 in the wake of the depression to provide liquidity and aid to the mortgage market. It became a government sponsored enterprise in 1968, and shortly after, Freddie Mac was formed to compete with Fannie Mae to create a more efficient secondary market for mortgages. While not explicit, there has always been the presumption that both the guarantor function and debt of these GSEs had full backing of the U.S. government. Indeed, the GSEs' debt generally was priced marginally above the prevailing treasury rate.

Consider the investment function of the GSEs. For every $1 of mortgage-backed securities purchased with equity, there was a large amount of debt issued to purchase additional mortgage-backed securities. Figure 2.2 shows the book and market leverage ratios of the GSEs, measured as assets divided by equity, over the period 1993–2007. The extraordinary point to note is the access to very high leverage, given that the GSEs were investing in risky, relatively illiquid mortgage-backed securities. This provides an idea of the size of the implicit government guarantee. In fact, the literature has quantified the transfer from taxpayers to the GSEs to be in the billions of dollars even before the crisis ignited (see, for example Passmore, 2005; Lucas and McDonald, 2006).

The investment portfolio of the GSEs became markedly riskier through time as they began to load up on nonprime mortgages under pressure from Congress and the Clinton Administration. Successive Secretaries of Housing and Urban Development (HUD) mandated that the GSEs increase the share of mortgage loans and guarantees

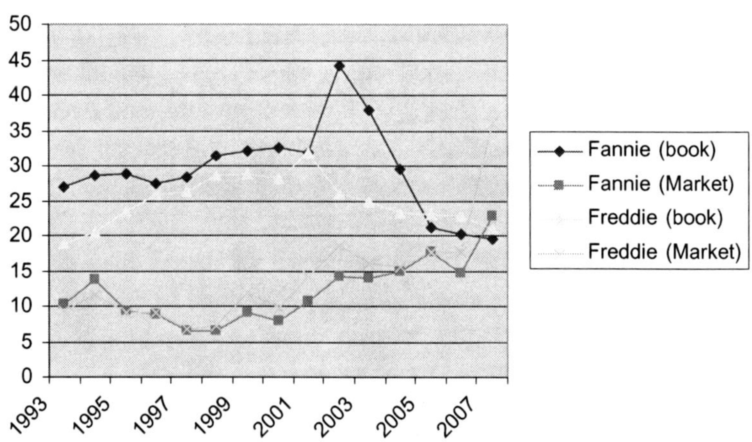

Fig. 2.2 The leverage ratio of the GSEs (1993–2007).

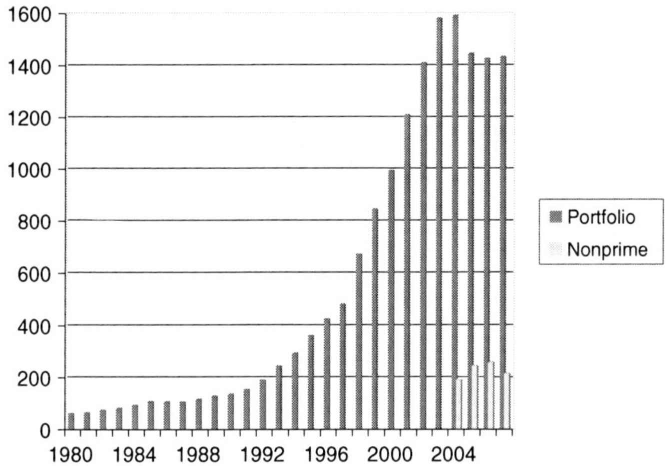

Fig. 2.3 The size of the GSE retained mortgage portfolio (in billions of $).

to low-income households to 50% and then 60% of their portfolios. Although some analysts have argued that the GSEs' non prime bets were much larger (Pinto, 2008), it is clear that by the mid 2000s at least 15% of the GSEs' funds were invested in subprime mortgages. In contrast to prime mortgages, however, these were not hedged using corresponding interest rate swaps. Figure 2.3 provides the size of the GSE mortgage portfolios, noting the rise in subprime holdings over the later years. Of course, with the lack of market discipline due to the government's guarantee, one would expect that the GSEs would invest in riskier assets to the extent possible. Quite apart from their politicized character, it is therefore not surprising that, as nonprime mortgages took off, the GSEs substituted risk toward these assets. The hybrid nature of the GSEs and the implied sovereign guarantee, in short, underlay a financial disaster waiting to happen.

To summarize, the traditional role of banks together with the limits imposed on them by Glass-Steagall led to relative calm in the U.S. financial system for fifty or so years after the 1930s. Once the Glass-Steagall barriers were lifted, the only real protection for the financial system was capital requirements and appropriate pricing of government guarantees covering individual financial institutions. With little or no pricing of government guarantees, the only remaining obstacle to increased risk-taking and systemic exposure was capital requirements. As we argue in Section 3, the financial crisis of 2007–2009 is centered on how LCFIs and other Wall Street firms exploited loopholes in regulatory capital requirements to take on an under-capitalized \$2–3 trillion highly leveraged, one-way asymmetric bet on the economy, particularly tied to residential real estate but also involving commercial real estate and consumer credit.

3

The New Banking Model of Manufacturing Tail Risk[1]

Given this background, we discuss the shift in the banking model during 2003–2Q 2007 compared to the traditional banking and securitization models.

The simple theory of banking is that banks act as financial intermediaries between depositors and borrowers (Diamond, 1984). Depositors provide funds to make loans, and banks provide expertise in assessing the creditworthiness of borrowers. Historically, then, the asset side of a bank's balance sheet (Figure 3.1) would consist of loans funded by deposits as well as loans funded by equity (and in general non-deposit debt).

A bank's loans are considered assets because they are owed to the bank by borrowers. Deposits are considered liabilities because, upon demand, they must be returned by the bank to the depositors. In the meantime, however, most deposits have been lent out to borrowers, with the exception of liquidity reserves, and the interest on these loans is the main source of the commercial bank's profits. Most deposits, therefore, are unavailable at any given time to be reclaimed by the depositors.

[1] This section draws heavily on the discussion in Acharya and Richardson (2009a).

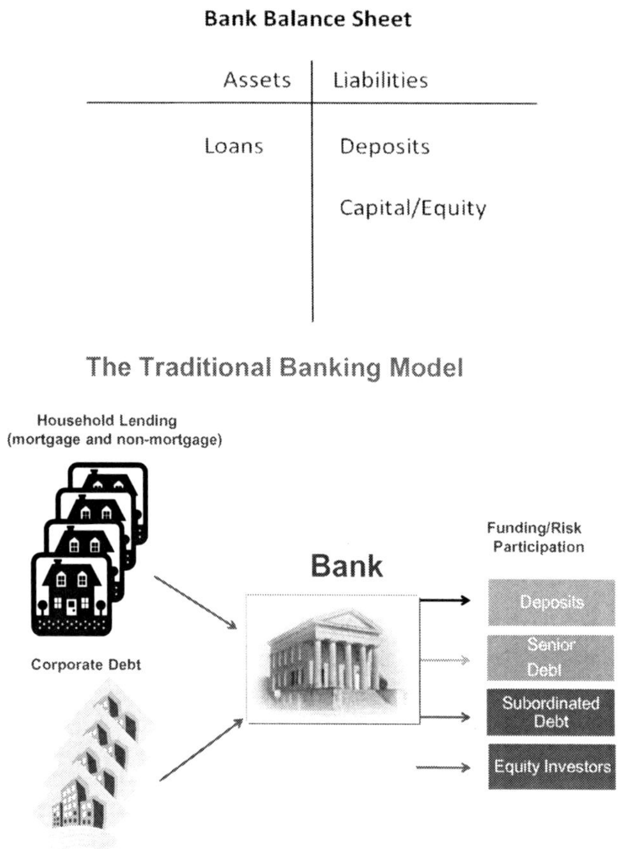

Fig. 3.1 Traditional banking.[2]

To avoid the possibility that all the depositors will demand the return of their deposits at the same time — as occurred during several panics between 1850 and 1914 and during the Great Depression — we have emphasized that deposits are generally insured up to a certain amount by the government. In return for this guarantee and an insurance fee, and to ensure that banks have a stake in the process, banks are required to hold a minimum amount of "capital" as a buffer against losses. Quite apart from simple prudence in management and

[2] We are grateful to Philipp Schnabl for schema describing the traditional bank balance sheet and its modern forms.

governance, even in the days of the Medicis in Florence or the Fugger in Frankfurt, banks that wanted to survive kept a sharp eye on capital adequacy. And while there are other complementary explanations of bank-capital regulation, this simple one suffices for exposition of our main point. For these purposes, what constitutes "capital" is defined by regulators. The regulations in place in the run-up to the crisis in most Western countries defined capital in terms of funds obtained either by raising equity (selling stock or certain forms of "hybrid" debt that has equity-like features), or by retaining earnings. We will shortly point out that banks' efforts to circumvent these capital-adequacy requirements caused the financial crisis.

In a world without deposit insurance, capital-adequacy regulations might in fact be unnecessary, as it often was in banking history. The creditors of financial institutions (depositors, uninsured bondholders, and other counterparties) would apply pressure to curb excessive risk taking. Uninsured bondholders and other counterparties could do this by charging higher interest rates to banks that took what seemed to be excessive risks. Similarly, depositors could demand higher interest rates on their deposits in exchange for the higher risk involved in using such banks. And if unanticipated risks seemed to arise in a given bank, they would take their money elsewhere, or under stress conditions participate in bank runs (akin to the run of unsecured creditors on banks during the ongoing crisis). But the creation of deposit insurance created a risk of moral hazard for traditional banks, and similarly, implicit government bailout guarantees for institutions that are considered too big to fail created moral hazard for today's LCFIs.

The bank-capital regulations of most Western countries follow the terms recommended by the Basel Committee on Banking Supervision (BCBS) of the Bank for International Settlements in Basel, Switzerland. Under the Basel accords, banks must maintain at least an 8% capital buffer against a risk-adjusted measure of their assets, although there is considerable national discretion in the actual implementation of the Accord. For instance, in the United States the FDIC has interpreted "at least" 8% to mean 10% if a bank is to be designated "well-capitalized" (a designation that brings certain privileges such as lower deposit insurance premiums).

The two main forms of "capital," according to the Basel rules, are equity and retained earnings. Maintaining large capital buffers is costly from an economic standpoint since debt, especially if short-term and demandable, has market discipline role that cannot be served by the relatively passive nature of equity financing (Calomiris and Kahn, 1991; Diamond and Rajan, 2001). However, even maintaining socially efficient levels of capital can seem privately costly to bank management if their attention is focused on short-term accounting measures of performance such as return on equity (ROE). For instance, the capital can be lent out at risk-free interest rate whereas putting it away into illiquid and tail-risky assets can generate a carry over and above the risk-free rate. While the return on both forms of investment should be similar on a risk-adjusted basis, the absence of proper accounting of risks in recording of profits can make reducing capital, that is, increasing leverage, highly attractive from the standpoint of generating greater ROE over the next quarter.

As such, in difficult times, if a bank's capital must be boosted through issuing equity shares, it generally signals to investors the adverse news that retained earnings are unlikely to be sufficient to meet the bank's capital needs (Myers and Majluf, 1984), and the new equity injections will dilute the value of existing shares (Myers, 1977) since the primary benefit of the injections accrues to creditors. It would seem that such costs of capital issuance might discipline banks and induce them to manage capital in a countercyclical manner. However, once decision-making horizons are shortened due to focus on quarterly accounting measures of performance with poor risk-adjustment of recorded profits, such dynamic and long-term incentives are lost.

Regardless of the exact nature of this cost, in order to deal with holding costly capital on balance sheet in originating assets, the model of banking evolved to focus on securitization (Figure 3.2). This allowed banks to avoid holding costly capital by essentially turning them into underwriters that continued to originate loans but then sell them off to others. Once loans are removed from a bank's balance sheet in this way, the 10% capital reserve need not be held.

Securitization explains the fact that there are far fewer deposits in the modern financial system than there are bank loans. The U.S.

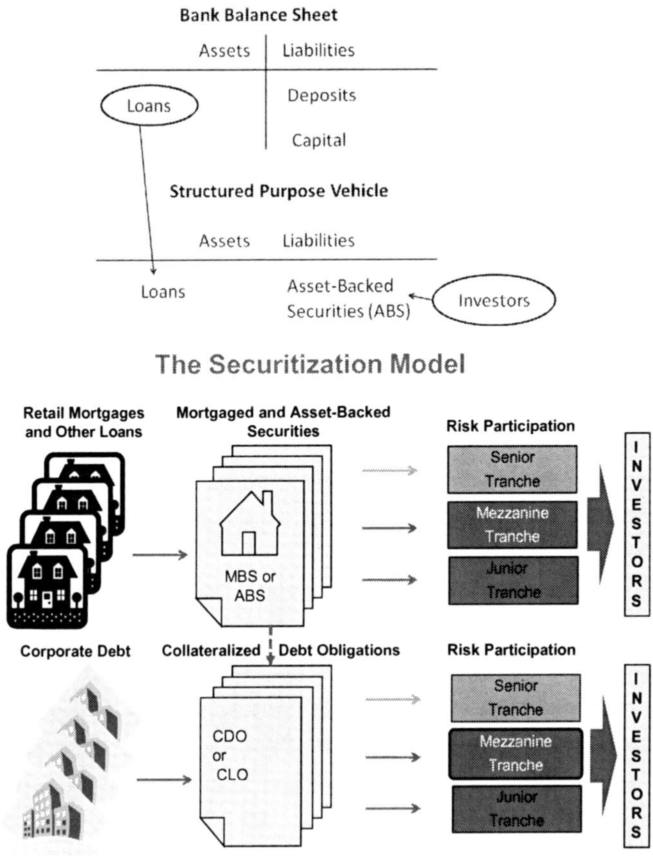

Fig. 3.2 Modern banking — securitization with risk transfer.

banking system currently holds approximately \$7 trillion in deposits, but the credit market includes \$2.7 trillion in bank and leveraged loans, \$3.3 trillion in commercial mortgages, \$1.3 trillion in subprime mortgages, \$5.8 trillion in non-agency (i.e., non-Fannie Mae or non-Freddie Mac) prime residential mortgages, and \$2.6 trillion in consumer loans, among others. The riskier credits, such as high-yield corporate loans, nonprime mortgages, commercial mortgages, and consumer credit, are likewise generally securitized.

With securitization, the original idea of banking is altered. Banks are now intermediaries between borrowers and *investors* (rather than just depositors). To understand how this works, consider the successful model of securitizing prime mortgages. This involves pooling prime mortgages into mortgage-backed securities (MBSs) that pay their owners fractional streams of the interest and principal payments collectively made by the mortgage holders. The principal and interest of these mortgages are guaranteed by Fannie Mae and Freddie Mac. The U.S. residential mortgage market is worth more than $10 trillion. Over 55% of it is securitized, and 64% of these securities are backed by Fannie and Freddie.

Toward the end of 2002, as credit markets began to recover from the recession of 2001, banks extended the prime-mortgage securitization model to other, riskier asset classes. This allowed banks to transfer these risks from their balance sheets to the broader capital market, including pension funds, hedge funds, mutual funds, insurance companies, and foreign-based institutions.

The new asset-backed securities were "structured," meaning that they divided (for example) mortgage pools into "tranches" according to the predicted riskiness of the loans. Holders of shares in the riskier tranches received higher interest payments, but in exchange, they were subject to losses before the holders of shares in the less-risky tranches suffered losses. Thus, the holders of the least-risky tranches, as determined by the three rating agencies — Moody's, Standard and Poor's, and Fitch — got a lower risk-based interest payment, but they would feel any effect of nonperformance in the structured security only after its "subordinated tranches" had stopped performing (through delinquency or default). The relatively low risk level of a AAA-rated tranche, however, did not necessarily mean that it was backed by prime loans. It might only mean that, of the thousands of nonprime loans in a given mortgage-backed security, this tranche was designated as the one that would continue to throw off income and principal income from performing debts in the entire security until all the other tranches had stopped performing.

In order to meet the demand for AAA-rated paper beyond that available from the top tranches of asset-backed securities, the mezzanine tranches of those structured could be packaged into collateralized debt obligations, which in turn could be tranched to create more

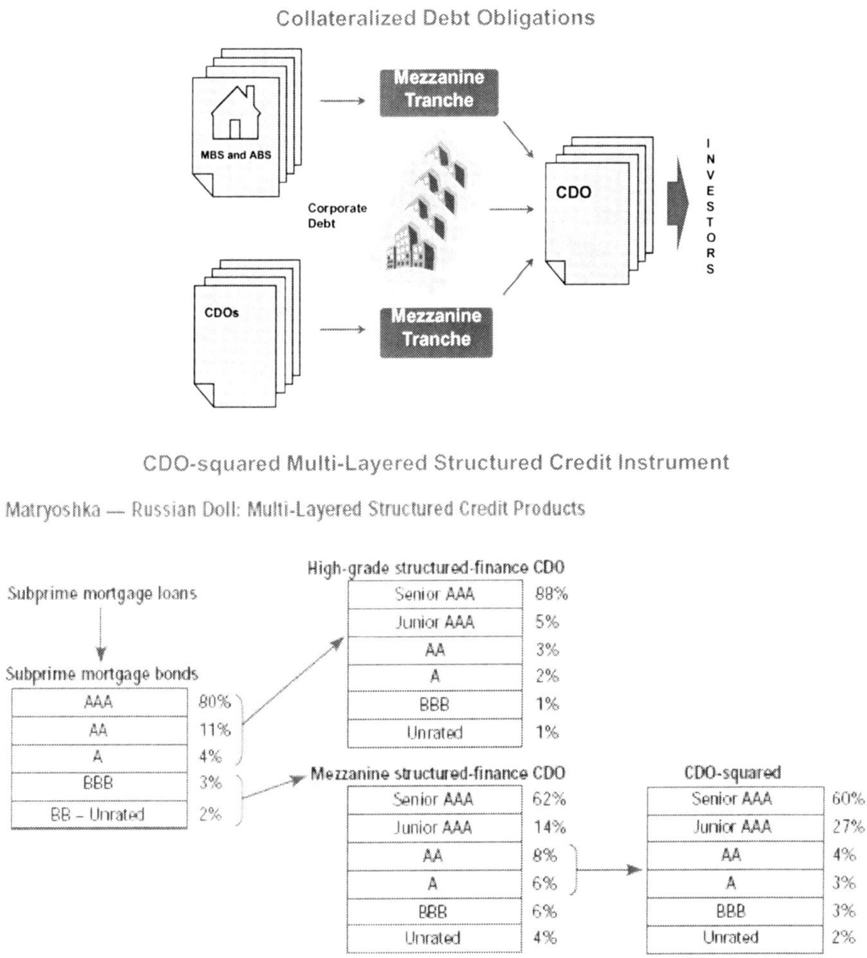

Fig. 3.3 Manufacturing CDOs and CDO-squareds.
Source: IMF staff estimates.
Note: CDO- collateralized debt obligation.

AAA-rated securities, and this could be repeated for the mezzanine tranches of CDOs in the form of CDO-squared issues (Figure 3.3).

The growth in structured securities across Wall Street during 2002–2007 was staggering. While residential mortgage-related securities were certainly a large component of the total, so too were securities backed by such assets as commercial mortgages, leveraged loans, corporate bonds, and student loans. Figure 3.4 graphs the new issuance of

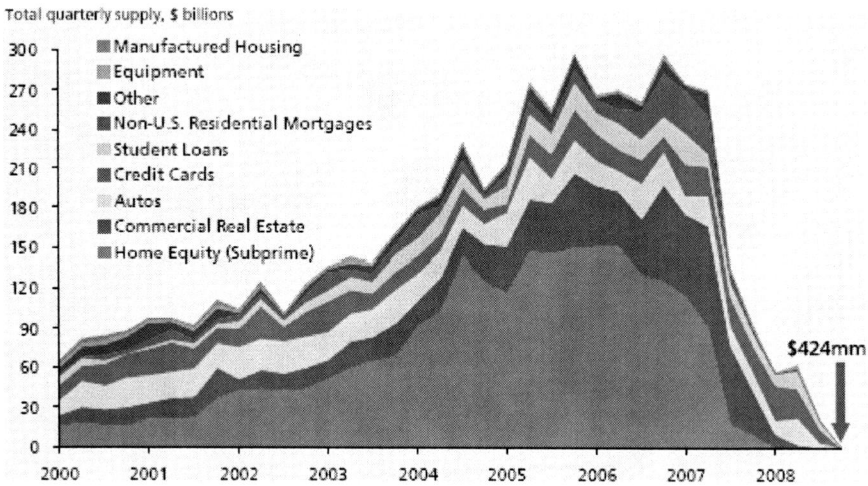

Fig. 3.4 Asset-backed security issuance, 2000–2008.

various asset-backed securities during this period. Note that there is an almost threefold increase in new issuance from 2002 to 2007. In the aggregate, securitization worldwide went from $767 billion at the end of 2001 to $1.4 trillion in 2004 to $2.7 trillion at the peak of the "bubble", in December of 2006. By late October 2008, the market had effectively collapsed.

It is very clear that the strongest demand for these asset-backed financial products came through the creation of "highest quality" — supposed to be essentially riskless — securities, which appealed to a host of potential investors such as pension funds, insurance funds, and money market funds. Interestingly, and crucially for our thesis, however, end investors were not the chief purchasers of these securities, and, in turn, of the underlying risks that were being securitized. In fact, the banks themselves, instead of acting as intermediaries between borrowers and investors by transferring the risk from mortgage lenders to the capital market, became primary investors. In addition to normal "pipeline" exposure to assets in the process of origination, securitization and distribution, they took on "warehousing" exposure by holding onto them (see Figure 3.5). Since — unlike a typical pension fund, fixed income mutual fund, or sovereign wealth fund — banks are

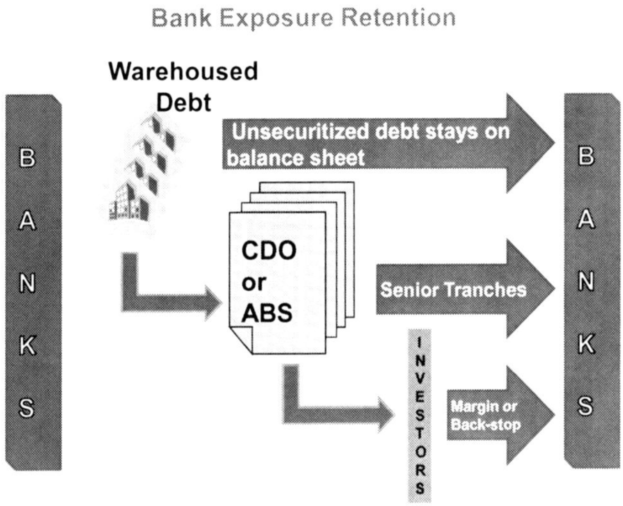

Fig. 3.5 Warehousing and retention of risks during asset-backed security issuance.

highly leveraged, this investment strategy was exceedingly risky. The goal, however, was logical — to create return on equity through the carry of asset-backed securities and simultaneously avoid minimum-capital regulations.

One of the two principal means for this "regulatory arbitrage" was the creation of off-balance-sheet special-purpose vehicles, which held onto many of the asset-backed securities. These vehicles were generically called "conduits." Structured investment vehicles (SIVs), which have received the most public attention, were one type of conduit.

With securitized loans placed in conduits rather than on a bank's balance sheet, the bank did not need to maintain capital against them. However, the conduits funded the asset-backed securities by issuing asset-backed commercial paper (ABCP) — short-term debt instruments sold in the financial markets, notably to investors in money market instruments. To be able to sell the ABCP, a bank would have to provide the buyers, i.e., the banks' "counterparties," with *guarantees* of the underlying credit — essentially bringing the risk back onto the banks themselves, even though that risk was not shown on their balance sheets (Acharya and Schnabl, 2009). This "new" banking model is depicted in Figure 3.6.

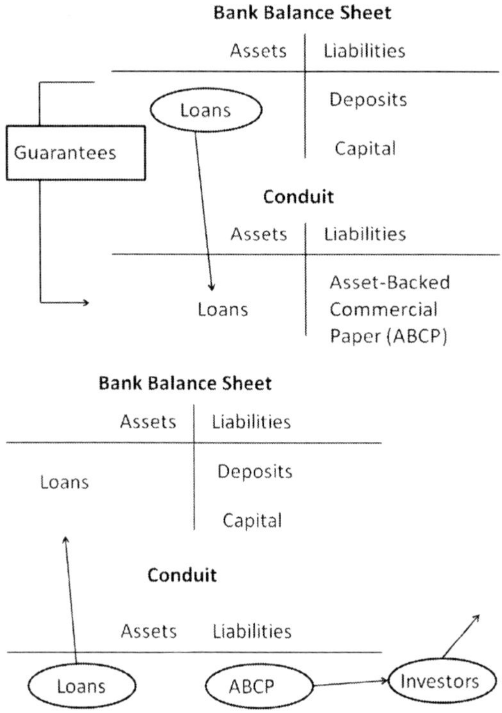

Fig. 3.6 Modern banking+ : securitization without risk transfer using ABCP conduits.

These guarantees had two important effects. First, guaranteeing the risk to banks' counterparties was essential in moving these assets off the banks' balance sheets. Designing the guarantees as "liquidity enhancements" of less than one year maturity (to be rolled over each year) allowed the banks to exploit a loophole in Basel capital requirements. The design effectively eliminated the "capital charge", so that banks achieved a tenfold increase in leverage for a given pool of loans. Second, the guarantees ensured the highest ratings for the off-balance sheet vehicles from the rating agencies. Indeed, the AAA ratings made it possible for banks to sell ABCP to money-market funds, which are required by law to invest mainly in AAA-rated securities. This allowed banks to fund the ABCP at low interest rates, similar to that paid on deposit accounts.

Figure 3.7 graphs the growth and collapse of the ABCP market over the years 2001 to 2009. ABCP issuance peaked from 2004 until

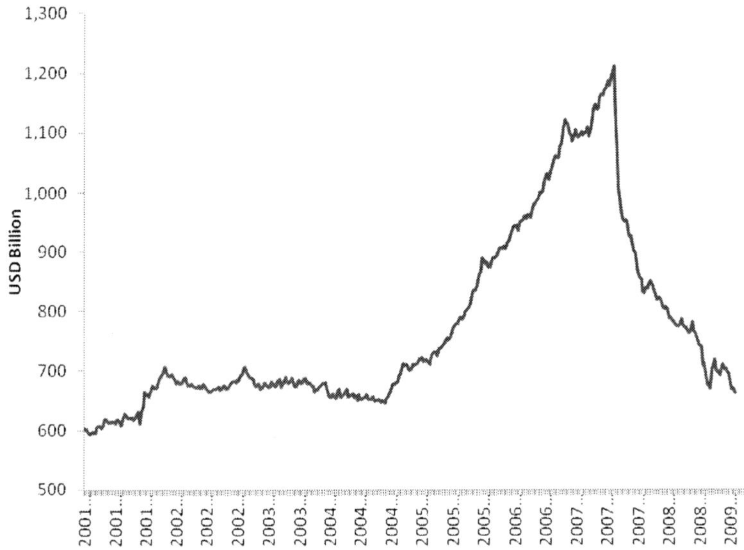

Fig. 3.7 Asset-backed commercial paper around the financial crisis of 2007–2009. *Source*: Federal Reserve Board. Data do not include European ABCP.

the second quarter of 2007. When the collapse occurred in the next quarter, Figure 3.8 shows that the cost of issuing ABCP rose from just 15 basis points over the Federal Funds rate to over 100 basis points (at its peak being close to 150 basis points). Consequently the ABCP could no longer be rolled over, and the banks had to return the loans to their balance sheets. Acharya et al. (2009c) show that when the crisis hit, of the $1.25 trillion in asset-backed securitized vehicles, only 4.3% of the loss was structured to remain with investors. The remaining loss wiped out significant portions of bank capital and threatened banks' solvency.

Not all banks followed the conduit model, which financed off-balance-sheet assets through the sales of ABCP. Some chose an alternative route that had a similar effect. A bank would still make loans and move them from its balance sheet by securitizing them. But as Shin (2009) explains, the bank then turned around and reinvested in AAA-rated tranches of the same securitized products they (or other banks) had created (Figure 3.9). Because of their AAA ratings, these securities had a significantly lower capital requirement under Basel 2 arrangement. For commercial banks, the Basel accord weighted the

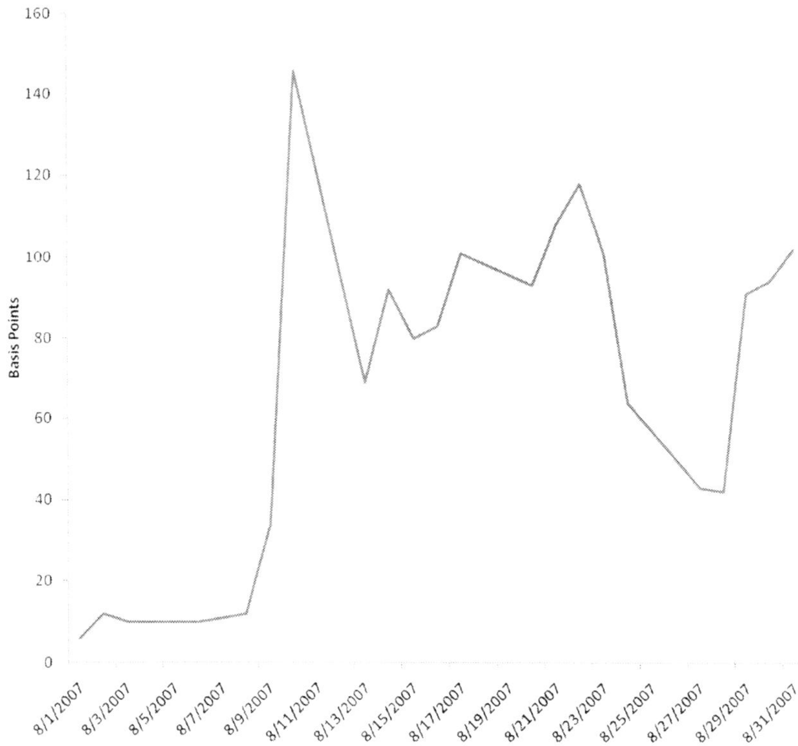

Fig. 3.8 The behavior of asset-backed commercial paper (ABCP) spread over the Federal funds rate during 2007.
Source: Federal Reserve Board.

risk of AAA-rated securities at half the risk of ordinary commercial or mortgage loans, and thus required an even lower capital reserve for them (20% risk weight compared to 50% for mortgages and 100% for corporate bonds). In 2004, the Securities Exchange Commission (SEC) granted stand-alone American investment banks the ability to employ internal models to assess credit risk and the corresponding capital charge. This allowed them even higher leverage than commercial banks, which duly skyrocketed from 22:1 debt to equity ratio to 33:1 within just three years.

As Table 3.1 shows, banks, GSEs (Fannie and Freddie), and broker/dealers in 2007 held $789 billion of the AAA-rated CDO tranches that were backed by nonprime loans, or approximately 50% of the volume

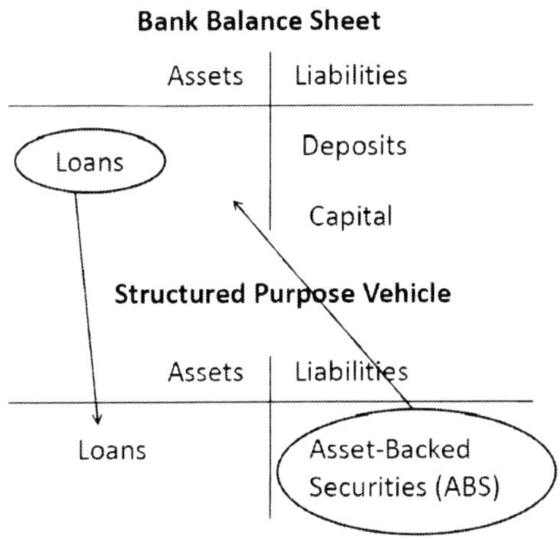

Fig. 3.9 Modern banking+ : originate, distribute and buy back.

Table 3.1. Holdings of mortgage-related debt by financial institutions (2007).

Type of financial institutions	Loans	HELOC*	Agency MBS	Non-Agency AAA	CDO subord.	Non-CDO subord.	Total	Percentage of outstanding volume
Banks and Thrifts	2,020	869	852	**383**	90		4,212	39%
GSEs and FHLB	444		741	**308**			1,493	14%
Brokers/dealers			49	**100**	130	24	303	3%
Financial Guarantors		62			100		162	2%
Insurance Companies			856	**125**	65	24	1,070	10%
Overseas			689	**413**	45	24	1,172	11%
Other	461	185	1,175	**307**	46	49	2,268	21%
Total	2,925	1,116	4,362	**1,636**	476	121	10,680	
	27%	10%	41%	**15%**	4%	1%		

Source: Krishnamurthy (2008).

outstanding at the time. Moreover, the majority of the subordinated tranches of the CDOs were also held by banks, broker/dealers, and monoline insurers (which insure only one type of bond — e.g., municipal bonds). They collectively held \$320 billion of the \$476 billion total outstanding.

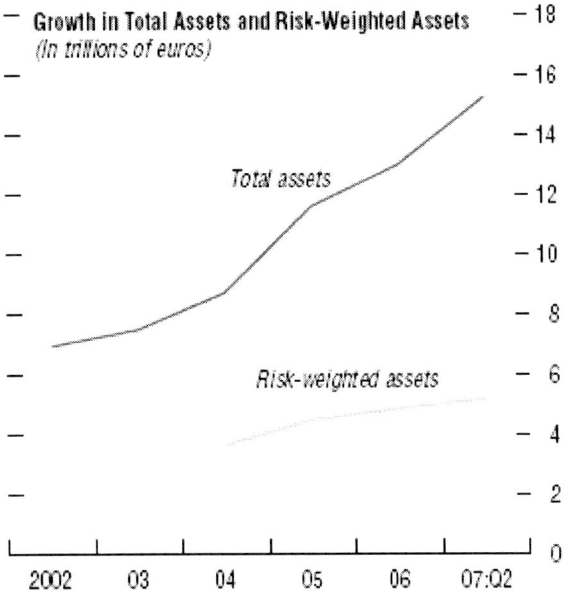

Fig. 3.10 Trends in bank assets, nature of assets and leverage.
Source: International Monetary Fund Global Financial Stability Report, April 2008.

To recap — while the assets on banks' balance sheets doubled between 2004 and the middle of 2007, the regulatory assessment of the risk of these assets grew at a far slower pace. As a result, banks were considered by the regulators to have been investing in relatively safe assets over this period because the assets were rated AAA. This enabled banks to double their leverage, and hence the quantity of profitable loans they could make. Figure 3.10 shows this trend in the quantity of total assets of top ten publicly traded banks relative to the trend in the quantity of their *risk-weighted* assets.

Why did the banks create, securitize, and then retain the risks associated with highly systematic and long-term assets such as subprime mortgages?

Take the AAA-rated tranches of subprime CDOs. True, they were risky. But banks that held these tranches had it both ways: On the up side, they reduced their capital requirements, and they (or other investors) earned the higher premium commanded by the risky nature of subprime loans. For example, at the peak of the housing bubble, in

June 2006, even the relatively low-yield AAA-rated tranches of subprime CDOs offered twice the premium of the typical AAA credit default swap of a corporation. On the down side, losses would only occur if a large number of subprime mortgages got hit at once, in which case even the AAA tranche of a CDO got hit. If such a rare event actually occurred, however, it would almost surely result from an economic catastrophe — a systemic shock affecting all markets at the same time.[3] The banks were betting their futures that this would not happen, or that the decision makers' time horizons were too short for them to care if it did happen. Of course, bad things do happen.

To get some understanding of how hard the systemic shock hit the AAA tranches, of asset-backed securities and their derivatives, Figure 3.11 graphs the various AAA-rated ABX index series from their initiation until the end of 2008 — an index of 20 representative CDOs of subprime mortgages. Such indices are initially priced at par, and

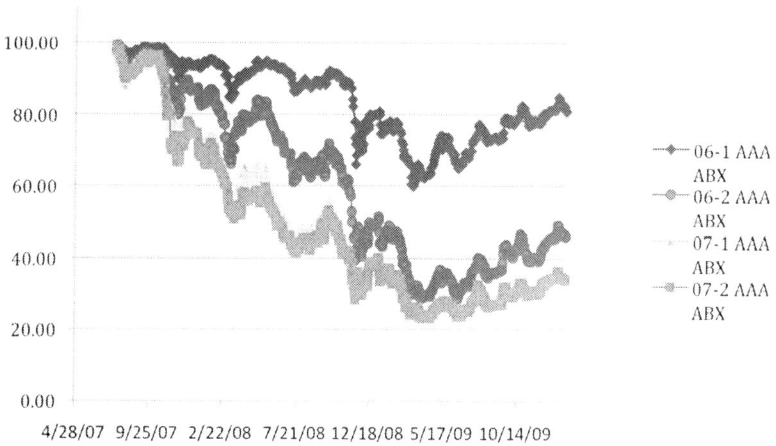

Fig. 3.11 Subprime Mortgage AAA-Tranche Pricing (2007–Jan 2010). (*Source*: Markit). *Source*: Markit. The Figure tracks the prices, from January 1, 2007 to February 17, 2010 of the ABX index of AAA tranches of mortgage-backed securities issued in the first and second halves of 2006 and 2007. The ABX index is an index of 20 representative collateralized debt obligations (CDOs) of subprime mortgages. The AAA tranche index represents an initial equally weighted portfolio of the AAA tranches of each CDO.

[3] Coval et al. (2008), therefore, call these kinds of tranche products "economic catastrophe bonds".

one can see that the 2006 series stayed around that level until late July 2007, when the crisis got underway. Depending on the series, the AAA tranches were selling from 20 cents to 80 cents on the dollar as of May 2009. Putting aside issues specific to the pricing of the ABX, at the borrowing costs shown in Figure 3.8 and given the aforementioned $789 billion of exposure, losses to the financial sector at the time ranged from $158 to $473 billion on their holdings of the AAA tranches of mortgage-backed securities alone.

Similarly, the financial firms that used off-balance-sheet conduits had, through the guarantees they issued on the ABCP, written huge quantities of insurance against a systemic decline in the overall economy, especially in the housing market. In the case of both AAA tranches and conduits, the guarantees were often provided by third-party insurers such as monolines and other insurers. Most prominently AIG, which also tried to have it both ways — they collected insurance premia when times were good, and would have to honor their promises only when there was a systemic decline of markets and the economy.

Effectively, the entire financial sector was riding a massive one-way bet on the economy. Commercial banks, through ABCP guarantees, and investment banks and insurance companies, through AAA-rated tranches and insurance on the tranches, had set up a way to (1) sell deep out-of-the-money (OTM) options, (2) with sector concentrations primarily on housing — a highly systematically risky and long-term asset, and (3) funded with short-term debt finance such as ABCP in case of conduits set up by commercial banks and unsecured commercial paper in case of investment banks. This intricate structure ensured that banks had a "carry" — both due to term premium in funding long-term assets with short-term debt and as a result of the systematic risk imbedded in the underlying mortgages. This carry can be alternately viewed as the price obtained by selling OTM options. And in this case, the options were structured with the aid of securitization in a way so as to arbitrage or optimize regulatory capital requirements. In aggregate, banks were not holding sufficient capital against the contingency that the tail systemic risk would materialize. The aggregate systemic exposure was hair-raising. During the period 2003-2007, banks used an accounting-based notion of profits that did not suitably correct for the long-run risk and return involved in selling OTM options. Consequently, they seemed enormously profitable. Regulatory capital levels seemed remarkably healthy. And there was little information on the exact nature of bets taken. Few asked the key question, "why are we so lucky?"

They soon found out with a vengeance when housing prices collapsed in 2007, the over-leveraged financial sector experienced a large solvency shock, and the real economy experienced the most severe financial crisis since the Great Depression. Specifically, the collapse of the ABCP market in the third quarter of 2007 forced commercial banks to bring the assets held in their conduits back onto their balance sheets or otherwise support them. This hit banks like Citigroup particularly hard and consumed Royal Bank of Scotland (which inherited the legacy of ABN Amro's conduits). Investment banks, which were not subject to the same capital requirements, held their CDOs on their books — but since investment banks, too, were typically funded overnight, they suffered the same maturity mismatch as did the commercial banks' off-balance-sheet conduits. By September 2008, investment-banking operations that had loaded up on AAA tranches of subprime mortgage-backed securities and their derivatives had effectively brought down UBS, Bear Stearns, and Lehman Brothers and threatened Merrill Lynch and Morgan Stanley.

While the post-Lehman phase has been the most difficult period of the crisis so far, in fact the first signs of the impending crisis can be traced nearly two years prior, with the bankruptcy of Ownit Solutions, a nonbank specialist in subprime and Alt-A (not-quite-prime) mortgages. From that point onward, there was a slow run on other non-bank nonprime mortgage lenders. Most of their loans were hybrid "2/28" or "3/27" adjustable-rate mortgages. These loans offered a fixed "teaser" rate for the first two or three years, and then adjustable rates for the remaining maturity of the mortgage. After the first two or three years, the adjustment of rates would be substantial enough to be unaffordable for subprime borrowers, so from the beginning the mortgages were designed to be refinanced. But for the most part, this would be possible for subprime borrowers only if the collateral on the loan (i.e., the price of the house) had increased in value. Otherwise, they would be forced into default.

Because most of these mortgages were all originated around the same time, mortgage brokers and lenders had inadvertently created an environment that could lead to a systemic wave of defaults if the price of housing declined two or three years later, when the mortgages were scheduled to reset (Ashcraft and Schuermann, 2008; Gorton, 2008). Once the failure of lenders like Ownit Solutions (and major banks with U.S. sub-prime businesses like HSBC) signaled that this had begun to happen, the short-term finance available to nonprime lenders dried up, and hundreds of specialists failed. The next wave of the crisis began on August 9, 2007, when three investment funds that were part of BNP Paribas, the French LCFI, could not determine the mark-to-market values of their securitized investments backed by subprime mortgages. This led to a suspension of redemptions by BNP Paribas, which in turn caused the asset-backed commercial paper market for conduits to "freeze-up." Purchasers of ABCP suddenly realized that assets backing the conduits were of such dubious quality that they might have little or no resale value, especially if they were all hit simultaneously with delinquencies and defaults (Acharya et al., 2008).

A year later, most of the assets funded by banks through securitized markets were hit by the same doubts, which ultimately brought down the investment banks that repackaged and warehoused subprime and other mortgages — as well as corporate, auto, and other loans — into structured securities. The failure of the likes of Bear Stearns and Lehman Brothers, which invested heavily in the securities created from these mortgages, led to severe counterparty risk concerns that paralyzed capital markets (and even interbank lending markets) and thus caused the worldwide recession. Standing behind the mortally wounded wholesale banks was the systemic failure of securitization market, triggered by the popping of the overall housing bubble. And this in turn had been fueled by the ability of these firms, as well as commercial banks, to finance so much housing stock in the first place. The severity of the resulting recession and its worldwide scope has been magnified by the massive decline in lending by commercial banks, including most of the major names such as BNP Paribas, Citigroup, Royal Bank of Scotland, and UBS, as well as Bank of America, JPMorgan, and others, such as Wachovia, that no longer exist. Contrary to the originate-and-distribute model, it was these same banks that turned out to be the main credit destinations for the mortgages originated by subprime lenders.

To summarize the genesis of it all, the root cause of the crisis was the desire of highly leveraged LCFIs to take even greater risks, generating even higher short-term "profits" than those associated with their role as financial intermediaries. They managed to do so by financing long-term, systematically risky assets such as mortgages using short-term, often overnight, debt. They further enhanced the "carry" by repackaging the risk in such a way as to get around the capital requirements imposed by regulators. This was the "new model" of LCFIs during 2003–2007 — to manufacture and take on systemic risk or write deep out-of-the-money options, but do so with little capital on the balance-sheet — which ultimately led to the financial crisis of 2007–2009.

4

Alternative Explanations of the Financial Crisis

There is no shortage of proximate causes of the financial crisis. We consider each of these in turn, and explain why most of them do not suffice to explain the spectrum of evidence available on what caused the financial crisis

1. *Moral hazard in the originate-and-distribute model*: A commonly mentioned cause of the crisis has been that the originate-and-distribute model of banking — the securitization model — destroyed incentives of loan originators, which led to the origination and distribution of poor quality mortgages. The conceptual point goes back at least to the work of Stiglitz (1992). For instance, in the buildup to the most recent crisis, there were mortgages granted to people with little ability to pay them back, and mortgages designed to systemically default or refinance in just a few years, depending on the path of house prices. There was the securitization of these mortgages, which allowed credit markets to grow rapidly, but at the cost of some lenders having little "skin in the game" and in turn contributing to the deterioration in loan quality (Dell'Ariccia et al., 2008; Mian and Sufi, 2008; Berndt and Gupta, 2008; Keys et al., 2008). Finally, opaquely structured securitized mortgages were classified AAA by rating agencies prone to modeling failures

and possible conflicts of interest between thorough risk assessment and generating fee income from security issuers

Perhaps surprisingly, these are not the ultimate reasons for the near-collapse of the financial system. If bad mortgages sold to investors hoodwinked by AAA ratings were all there was to it, those investors would have absorbed their losses and the financial system would have moved forward. Although numerous investors would have been burned, the crash would have been no different, in principle, than the bursting of the tech bubble in 2000. In other words, the failure of the originate-and-distribute model might help explain why we saw poor quality mortgages, but it fails to explain why the mortgage risk ultimately did not leave the financial intermediaries responsible for originating and distributing them.

Since the AAA ratings indicated to investors that these tranches of "asset-backed" investments — collateralized debt obligations (CDOs) and collateralized loan obligations (CLOs) — were as safe as the safest possible non-sovereign debt instruments, the role of the rating agencies in this process should not be underestimated (White, 2006). Nevertheless, we believe that the rating agencies' role *in marketing asset-backed securities to investors* can be overstressed as a factor in the crisis because, in fact, investors were not the chief purchasers of these securities — the financial intermediaries or banks themselves were, as shown convincingly in Table 3.1. To repeat, instead of acting as intermediaries between borrowers and investors by transferring the risk from mortgage lenders to the capital market, the banks themselves became primary investors, and so it was not a true originate-and-distribute model that was at work but rather the new banking model of "originate-distribute-and-hold", incurring massive systemic tail risks that ultimately brought the financial sector down.

2. *Good securitization or bad securitization?* Gorton (2008, 2009) provides an explanation of the financial crisis based on the idea that financial intermediation is intrinsically about financial institutions selling risk-free instruments that are essentially informationally insensitive to investors. However, adverse risks can materialize in the future which may make these instruments sensitive to information relating to the underlying assets, in which case investors "run" in order to enhance

their redemption priority before other investors put in their claims and before there is a further deterioration of assets. This is the view that securitization growth during 2003–2007 was inherently of the "good" type and therefore economically beneficial. For instance, the creation of AAA-rated tranches could be characterized as supplying investors with informationally insensitive securities. The growth in the wholesale credit market — the "repo" transactions in which banks borrow from each other against treasuries or relatively high-quality assets, often on overnight basis — could also be viewed similarly in terms of creating liquidity flows that provide plumbing for securitized intermediation in the economy.

Gorton (2008, 2009) thus attributes the panic of 2007-09 as essentially a run on securitized banking — for instance, on the repo markets — due to the increase in risk in the underlying assets and counterparty risk among the financial intermediaries themselves. To Gorton's phraseology, these intermediaries were "slapped" by the invisible hands of the market suddenly recognizing that securities and transactions hitherto informationally insensitive had now turned informationally sensitive. As shown in Figure 3.7, the introduction of ABX indices tied to the quality of securities backed by U.S. subprime assets deteriorated steadily during the Summer of 2007 and ignited fatal runs on securitized banking

We do not contest the view that securitization can in principle be economically beneficial. Indeed, it seemed to have worked remarkably well until the most recent crisis erupted. We also do not dispute the view that a part of the financial crisis was a run on securitized banking. However, we have two fundamental points of departure from Gorton's "good securitization" view.

First, exposures of the financial sector to 50% of all AAA-rated sub-prime tranches, as shown in Table 3.1, is hard to square with the "good securitization" view. Securitization's purpose is to spread risks to end investors and away from the financial sector, rather than create "hot potatoes" (Shin, 2009) for circulation within the financial sector. Indeed, the classical theory of securitization (for example Gorton and Pennacchi, 1990) argues that intermediaries should sell most or all of the "risk-free" tranches and hold back the information-sensitive first-loss tranches, which is what often happened as the securitized sector developed. This is in striking contrast to the securitization model financial intermediaries adopted during 2003–2007, since they themselves held AAA-rated tranches. In terms used in international trade, they increased their focus on activities where they had a comparative disadvantage as against the informationally sensitive activities where they had a comparative advantage, which makes no sense.

Second, the structure of ABCP conduits can be viewed as potentially consistent with the traditional view of securitization. In this view, banks sell guarantees to conduits in order to issue highly rated, short-term ABCP. However, as explained earlier, the guarantees were in fact 100% and were un-priced. That is, what happened was "securitization without risk transfer" (Acharya et al., 2009c) and guarantees were structured in a way that reduced and effectively eliminated regulatory capital requirements.

Contrary to this explanation of the crisis, our view is that the growth in securitization during 2003–2007 was primarily of the "bad" type, in that it was directly contrary to the risk-transfer objective underlying traditional forms of securitization, and allowed banks to synthesize systemic tail risk without holding much capital against it.

3. *Global imbalances:* Many analysts of the financial crisis have singled out huge global imbalances as a primary cause of the crisis. Bernanke (2005) argued in a speech that the "savings glut" in Asia, most notably in China, and several European countries with current account surpluses such as Germany, had created severe and persistent global imbalances. These imbalances by and large found their way through capital flows into the U.S. economy (Caballero et al., 2008). Importantly, unlike capital flows to emerging markets, a large share of these flows was subsequently invested in effectively risk-free assets such as U.S. treasuries, U.S. agency debt, and money market fund shares. Some observers (for example Caballero and Krishnamurthy, 2009) have additionally argued that the appetite of surplus countries for risk-free assets left the US economy fragile by concentrating the real risks in its financial sector. Portes (2009), for example, recently wrote: "I maintain that global macroeconomic imbalances are the underlying cause of the crisis. ... The underlying problem in international finance over the

past decade has been global imbalances, not greed, poor incentive structures, or weak financial regulation, however egregious and important these may be". Combined, these observations form the global imbalance explanation of the financial crisis of 2007–2009.

It is certainly true that much capital has flowed to the United States. The reasons are many: (a) The U.S. dollar's status as the reserve currency; (b) The depth, liquidity, and relative safety of U.S. financial markets; (c) Relative demographic; and (d) Good institutions. The U.S. current account has been in deficit for 20 years and the size of the deficit has averaged more than 4% of GDP for at least ten years. But, it is very difficult to make a causal connection between capital flows and the financial crisis that is void of reliance on seeking of tail risks by LCFIs. The financial crisis seems to have arisen primarily due to this seeking of tail risks with capital flows linked to global imbalances having fueled that fire.

In particular, while global imbalances are clearly central to understanding the capital flows into the U.S. economy, they fall short in explaining the financial crisis on two different dimensions. First, they fail to explain why the risk-free assets — for example, the AAA-rated securities — found their way into the balance sheets of the U.S. financial institutions (as shown in Table 3.1) rather than simply ending up in the asset holdings of surplus countries.

Second, Acharya and Schnabl (2009) explain that the global imbalances hypothesis does not coincide with the geography of the financial crisis — in particular, why the crisis took such a global form right from its inception. Clearly financial institutions in the U.K. and the U.S., both deficit countries were the hardest hit in the crisis. But, financial institutions in Switzerland (UBS), the Netherlands (ABN Amro), and Germany (WestLB, Deutsch Bank), all surplus countries, were among the hardest hit. UBS was effectively a hedge fund that lost most of its capital in exposure to AAA-rated tranches of the U.S. subprime assets; ABN AMRO was one of the largest creators of off-balance sheet conduits with liquidity guarantee provisions backed by little capital. And indeed, the first banks to collapse in the crisis due to exposure to ABCP markets were in Germany, a surplus nation. In August 2007, IKB and Sachsen Bank had to be bailed out. These banks had experimented investing in subprime assets in search of a new model following the withdrawal (forced by the European Union competition authorities) of the state guarantees on their liabilities. Thus, simply relying on global imbalances to explain failures in the financial sector proves to be grossly inadequate.

Further, many countries with large deficits as a percentage of GDP, such as Australia, Spain, Italy, were unscathed. What was the difference between countries that were hit hard and those that were not? The difference appears to be in the choices the banks and LCFIs made about what to take onto their balances sheets and the regulatory systems in place. Acharya and Schnabl (2009) explain for example that in spite of the housing price crash, banks in Spain have been reasonably well-buffered due to the prudent capital charge applied to off-balance sheet conduits that have recourse to bank balance sheets and reserves-averaging in good times based on past asset growth (that served to restrict asset growth as well as create adequate capital buffers for a downturn affecting the quality of assets).

Figures 4.1 and 4.2 and Table 4.1 help illustrate these points. Table 4.1 in particular shows banks with the top ten exposures to ABCP conduits, relative to their equity capitalizations, as of January 2007. This can be viewed as the extent of poorly capitalized off-balance sheet assets that banks took on.

Table 4.1 shows that, of the top six banks, three were in surplus countries (WestLB and Deutsche Bank in Germany, ABN Amro in the Netherlands) and three were in deficit countries (HBOS in the UK, Société Générale in France, and Citibank in the United States), with the top two among these banks being WestLB and HBOS. Figure 4.1 shows that, indeed, the average measure of ABCP exposure to equity for countries is unrelated to whether they were surplus or deficit nations, and if anything the relationship is positive. Germany, Belgium, and Netherlands had the highest ABCP to equity exposure for banks in the period leading up to the crisis. Confirming this, Figure 4.2 shows that when the ABCP crisis broke out in August 2007, the average performance of banks at the country-level was again as bad for surplus nations as for deficit nations.

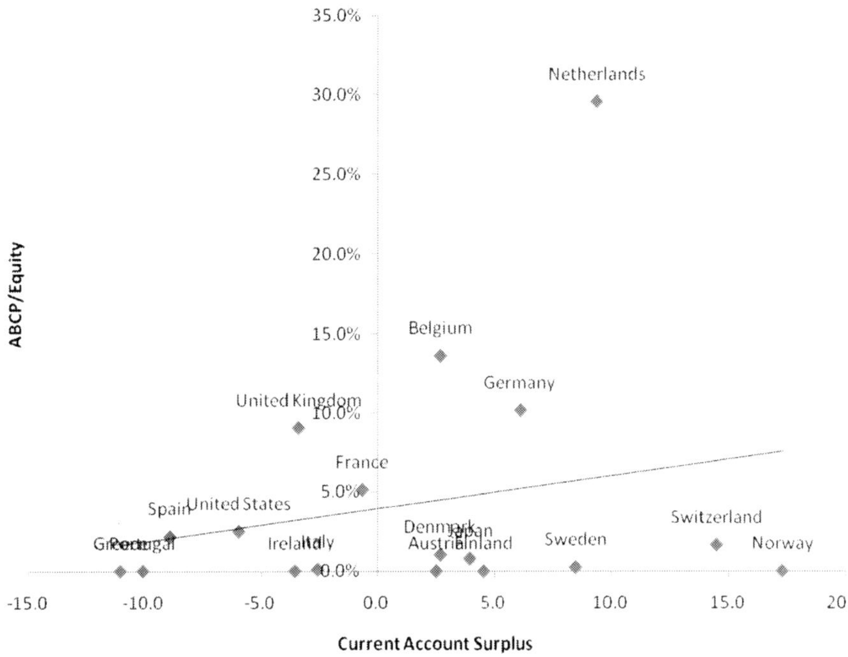

Fig. 4.1 ABCP and global imbalances, weighted by GDP.
(*Source*: Acharya and Schnabl (2009)).
This figure shows the correlation between global imbalances, measured as the Current Account Deficit in 2006, and off-balance sheet activity, measured as ABCP as of 1/1/2007 relative to country GDP in 2006. The current account deficit data is from the OECD Economic Outlook. The GDP country data is from the OECD Statistical Database measured at prices and exchange rates of 2000. The ABCP data is based on Moody's data and only includes ABCP sponsored by commercial banks.

In short, the financial crisis may have been largely based on dubious quality of assets in the deficit countries, but there was a great deal of direct exposure to ABCP guarantees sold to these assets among banks in surplus countries as well. Any explanation of the financial crisis must come to grips with the propensity of the banks in surplus countries to manufacture tail risk in this manner. Global imbalances help in understanding the flow of capital across countries, but in a world of integrated financial sectors, global banks of surplus countries can themselves be exposed if they are poorly regulated and have incentives to take on assets of poor quality (being financed elsewhere by the imbalances).

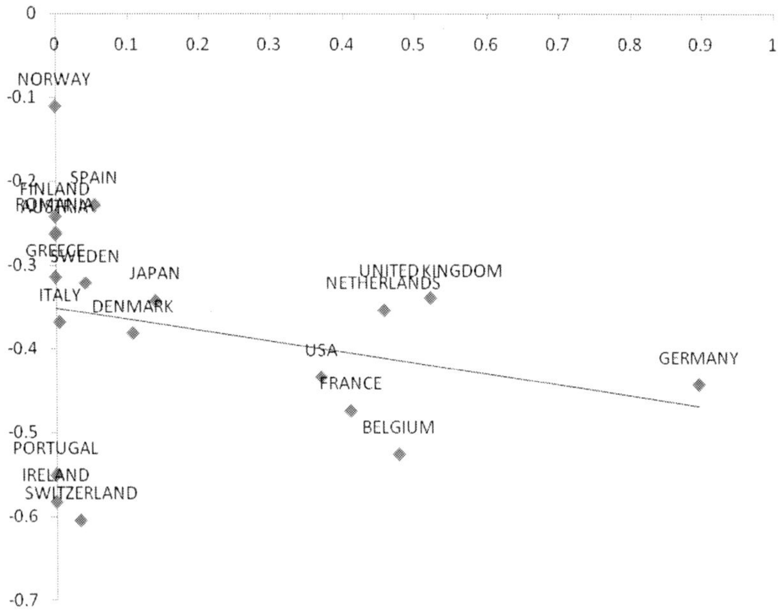

Fig. 4.2 Stock returns and ABCP from July 2007 to July 2008, by country. (*Source*: Acharya and Schnabl (2009)).
This figure shows the correlation between global imbalances, measured as the Current Account Deficit in 2006, and off-balance sheet activity, measured as the asset-weighted ABCP as of 1/1/2007 relative to equity per country. The current account deficit data is from the OECD Economic Outlook. The GDP country data is from the OECD Statistical Database measured at prices and exchange rates of 2000. The ABCP data is based on Moody's data and only includes ABCP sponsored by commercial banks.

Obstfeld and Rogoff (2009) present a more nuanced view that both the perpetuation of global imbalances and the occurrence of the financial crisis have common roots in loose monetary policies in the United States (and China's ability to maintain an underpriced currency), as discussed below. Note, however, that this common explanation — the loose monetary policy in the United States — fails in explaining the geography of the financial crisis, as outlined in Figures 4.1 and 4.2 and Table 4.1.

4. *Mis-pricing of risk: The "false" belief in the Great Moderation and the "animal spirits":* Akerlof and Shiller (2009) present perhaps the most authoritative endorsement of the view that there were strong psychological forces that led to the current financial crisis. They attribute

Table 4.1. Ten largest ABCP sponsors and their off-balance sheet leverage relative to equity.

	ABCP (bn)	Assets (bn)	Equity (bn)	ABCP/Equity
Citibank	93	1,884	120	77.4%
ABN Amro	69	1,301	34	201.1%
Bank of America	46	1,464	136	33.7%
HBOS	44	1,160	42	105.6%
JPMorgan Chase	42	1,352	116	36.1%
HSBC	39	1,861	123	32.1%
Societe Generale	39	1,260	44	87.2%
Deutsche Bank	38	1,483	44	87.8%
Barclays	33	1,957	54	61.5%
WestLB	30	376	9	336.6%

Source: Acharya et al. (2009c).

the crisis both to the blind faith in ever-rising house prices and correspondingly plummeting faith in capital markets once the house prices crashed. There was certainly a widely shared view among macroeconomists in the decade prior to the crisis that a so-called "Great Moderation" had become established, a period with a genuine fall in macroeconomic volatility due to development of global capital markets and the risk-sharing that it provided (Stock and Watson, 2002). This was reflected in a downward revision of asset price volatility as shown in Figure 4.3 for levels of VIX, a measure of market volatility implied from short-term (30-day) option prices on the S&P 500 stock index. VIX typically ranged above 20% per annum prior to 2003, but almost always remained between 10% and 20% until the Summer of 2007. Within two years, it had jumped to an unprecedented level of 80%.

Akerlof and Shiller (2009) and other proponents of behavioral explanations of the financial crisis attribute the housing and the credit market boom to a misplaced faith in a permanent downward shift in volatility, or to markets in general being excessively euphoric in good times and failing to impose sufficient discipline on risk-takers. In other words, the behavioral view of the financial crisis is simply that risks were mispriced and markets ignored early-warning signals that the housing market and the economy were overheated, fueling the boom instead through extraordinary valuations attached to both credit and equity instruments.

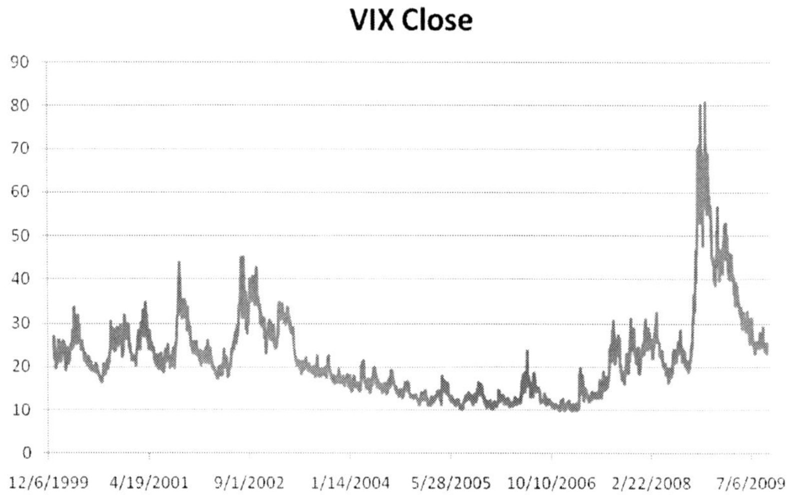

Fig. 4.3 Behavior of VIX, the option-implied measure of volatility during 2000–2009. (*Source*: Chicago Board Options Exchange).

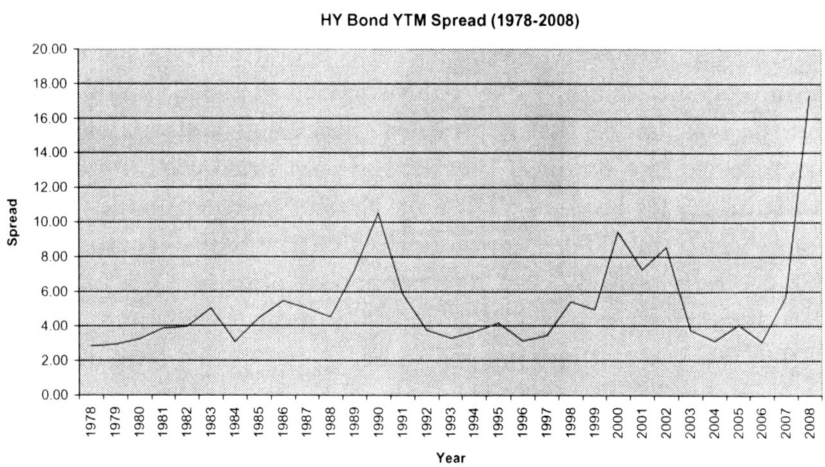

Fig. 4.4 Historical high yield bond spreads (1978–2008).
Source: Salomon Center, Stern School of Business, NYU.

Such a view is not entirely unwarranted. Figure 4.4, for instance, graphs the high-yield bond spread over Treasuries on an annual basis over the period 1978–2008. The lowest point in the graph, from June 1, 2006 onwards (not visible due to the annual nature of the data), is 260 basis points on June 12th 2007. This is remarkably close to the start of the crisis, indeed, just a few of weeks before Bear Stearn' hedge funds that invested in sub-prime securities ran into problems. As the graph shows, the high-yield bond spread was essentially hovering around its historical lows for most of 2004–2007, when the risks were in fact rising in the financial sector of the economy. Again, within two years, this spread jumped to the historic high of 1,800 basis points.

So why does the behavioral explanation fall short in explaining this particular episode? Note that housing assets cannot be easily short-sold. That is, a speculator wanting to express a negative view on the housing market cannot do so easily. Indeed, this became possible only a year prior to the crisis through development of trading in protection products on (ABX) indices linked to prices of asset-backed securities. Consequently, housing booms and busts are by and large a function of availability of credit in the economy. When there is a credit boom, housing prices rise substantially; and when there is a credit contraction, housing prices decline. It is imperative for the behavioral explanation to come to terms with reasons for and consequences of the credit boom and bust.

As explained in Section 3, the financial sector had undertaken highly sophisticated structures in order to buy mortgages from originators, securitize them, partly sell them, and hold the rest. If their own access to credit was very inexpensive or if they simply mispriced the risk of a housing crash, there would have been no need to increase their own leverage in funding the tremendous creation of housing finance that occurred. The financial sector had to simply expand its asset-base, and capital was readily available to do so (at abnormally low costs under the null of the behavioral hypothesis). But asset expansion was not simply a scaling-up of balance sheets. Instead, the asset expansion was associated with a rise in the leverage of financial institutions, in particular through design of clever guarantees sold to ABCP conduits and slicing and dicing of risks to create AAA-rated tranches, which in turn helped reduce capital requirements. Consequently, the picture that emerges from the evidence in Section 3 is one of a financial sector eager to take on excessive leverage even in a world where equity capital was easily available. Furthermore, there is something internally inconsistent about bankers getting it all wrong as far as price of risk is concerned and yet getting it all right as far as reduction of capital requirements is concerned.

Finally, the leverage undertaken by the financial sector was essentially reflective of a severe short-term bias. Again, as explained in Section 3, the leverage was constructed primarily through issuance of short-term asset-backed commercial paper (for commercial banks) or unsecured commercial paper (for investment banks). Since investors in such paper have the right to "run" on the issuing conduits or investment banks, the pricing of such debt is naturally dependent on short-term measures of volatility. Banks sponsoring conduits or holding the underlying long-term assets are, however, subject to short-term volatility. In particular, if risk rises, the short-term paper may not be rolled over and the shortfall would have to be met by bank capital. Since the risk-taking model of modern banking during 2004–2007 was built around constructing short-term carry and paying it out as profits, the long-run risks were ultimately ignored also by bank managers and their boards.

Figure 4.5 shows that the ratio of two-year implied volatility from S&P 500 option prices was on average 30–40% higher than the short-term one-month volatility over the period 2Q 2005–2Q 2007. This upward sloping term-structure of volatility is typical during boom periods, when short-term volatility is low and long-term volatility is high, and inverts itself during stress times (as can be seen in the figure after the onset of the crisis). As noted by Engle (2009), long-run volatility should incorporate the possibility that the level of risk may change over time — that is, rise from the current levels in boom times. This was indeed the case with market-observed long-term volatility. Hence, it is more likely that the financial sector at large ignored the long-term risks because it had incentives to do so, as discussed below.

All of this still begs the question why there were such abrupt shifts in the market price of risk when the crisis took hold in August 2007. We conjecture that since most risks undertaken by the banking sector were through opaque over-the-counter and off-balance sheet positions, investors did not have the relevant information that disclosed regulatory capital levels of banks did not mean what they implied. When its hedge funds invested in sub-prime assets had to be bailed out

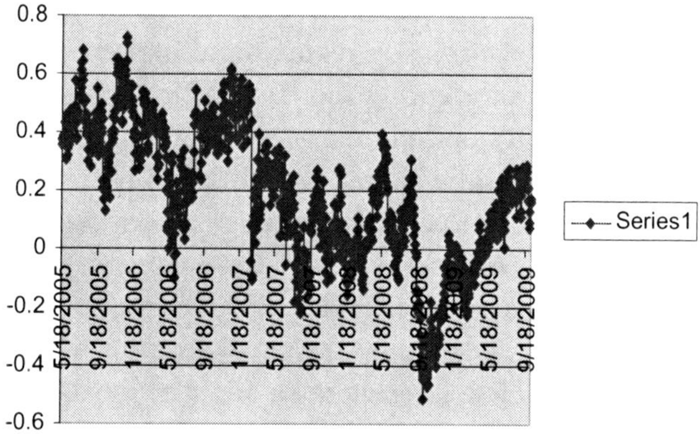

Fig. 4.5 Ratio of two-year at-the-money (ATM) S&P 500 implied volatility to one-month ATM volatility, i.e., $\sigma_{2\text{yr}}/\sigma_{1\text{mth}} - 1$
(*Source*: Bloomberg).

by Bear Stearns, and BNP Paribas' hedge funds suspended redemptions on August 8 2007, the absence of a market for selling sub-prime asset-backed securities made it clear to investors that the entire financial sector had taken a one-way bet on the economy. Since that day, markets have in fact been right about most failures (of the shadow banking world, leveraged hedge funds, Bear Stearns, Lehman Brothers, Wachovia, Washington Mutual, etc.) with the exception of A.I.G., whose collapse and rescue in September 2008 was a surprise to most observers. We conjecture that market's failure in picking up AIG's woes was most likely due to opacity arising from the completely over-the-counter (and thus, largely unregulated and often undisclosed) nature of its credit default swap positions. Regulatory arbitrage exposes markets to unexpected outcomes, and most likely played a destabilizing role during 2004–2009. It ultimately compromised market discipline in good times (2004–2Q 2007) producing low cost of credit, so that the correction that took hold on the release of hidden information (3Q 2007–2009) had to be larger and more severe.

5. *The Greenspan "put":* An important reason why asset-pricing bubbles may arise (even in the absence of "animal spirits") is due to the risk-shifting problem of leveraged households and financial institutions, coupled with the so-called "Greenspan put" — that when asset prices

(such as house prices) decline, interest rates will be lowered by the central bank. An expected future reduction of interest rates will tend to raise asset prices, exacerbating the risk-shifting problem associated with the limited liability option in leveraged financing of assets. Allen and Gale (2000) explain in a simple model that if borrowing costs are insensitive to risks (e.g., due to government guarantees or opacity), then asset-pricing bubbles arising due to loose monetary policy can, in the limit, be explosive in nature. Taylor (2009) argues that the counterfactual interest rates based on the "Taylor rule" during the period 2002–2005 far exceeded the low interest rates adopted by the U.S. Federal Reserve after the recession of 2001–2002 (see Figure 4.6). Taylor also shows that under this counterfactual, the housing price boom and bust that developed would probably not have materialized — "no boom, no bust". Obstfeld and Rogoff (2009) couple the loose monetary policy argument with global imbalances, implying that low interest rates in the United States allowed it to continue with its foreign borrowing at low rates to maintain its macroeconomic imbalances and avoid tough policy decisions concerning the fiscal deficit.

By and large, the role played by loose monetary policy in fueling the housing price bubble is hard to dispute. Indeed, U.S. monetary

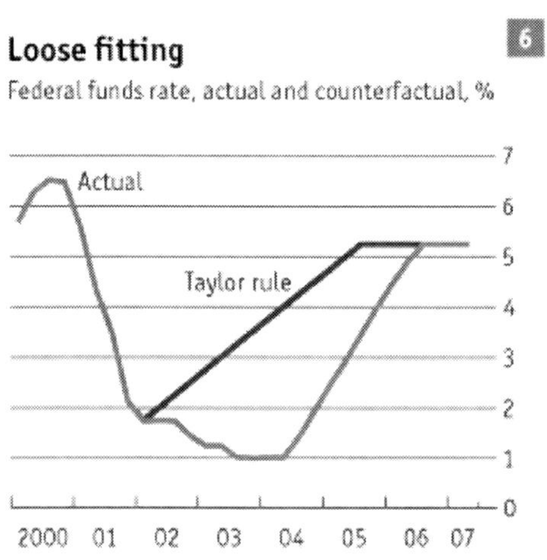

Fig. 4.6 Loose monetary policy of the United States (*The Economist*, 18 October 2007).

policy kept borrowing rates low not just for the households but also for the financial sector. Importantly, it made it attractive for banks from outside of the United States to borrow in U.S. dollars and fund asset purchases in the United States (Acharya and Schnabl, 2009). This does not necessarily explain why we ended up with a full-blown banking crisis, however. As we have stressed earlier, had the banks and LCFIs transferred the assets they created by lending down the quality curve — mainly sub-prime mortgages — on to end investors, even the large negative shock arising due to popping of the housing bubble would not have resulted in a significant financial crisis. Consequently, we view loose monetary policy during 2002–2005 as a primary candidate for sowing seeds of the economic crisis in the United States, whereas the tail risk-seeking, regulatory arbitrage motives of the LCFIs as the primary explanation for the financial crisis.

6. *Liquidity crisis or solvency crisis?* Finally, we consider the classic debate whether financial crises occur due to liquidity or solvency problems, in the context of this crisis. Allen and Gale (2007) build a series of economic models of financial crises in which depositors run on banks following the arrival of some adverse news about bank asset quality. The inability of banks to liquidate long-term assets at their fair values plays a crucial role in precipitating the crisis. Specifically, if the market among buyers of assets is segmented, or if there is not sufficient arbitrage capital set aside for asset purchases, then liquidation values reflect available cash in the market — Allen and Gale call this "cash-in-the-market" pricing — rather than fundamental values. In turn, the likelihood of such liquidations causes all depositors to run at once, since there will not be much long-run value in assets left post-liquidations. In other words, liquidity problems in the market for assets exacerbate the problem caused by adverse news about those assets.

Figure 4.7 shows that the market indeed had adverse information about asset quality. The figure graphs the demeaned value of the ratio of the Office of Federal Housing Enterprise Oversight (OFHEO) repeat-sale house price index to the Bureau of Labor Statistics (BLS) shelter index (i.e., gross rent plus utilities components of the CPI). Because of de-meaning, the average value of this ratio is zero. As is clear that

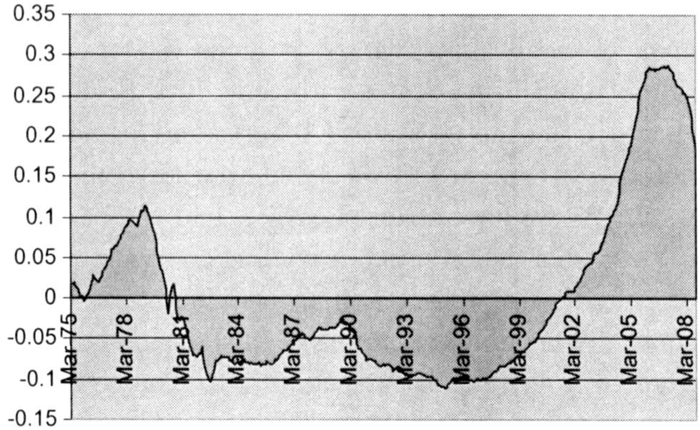

Fig. 4.7 House price to rent ratio (1975–2008).
Source: Own calculations, OFHEO, BLS.

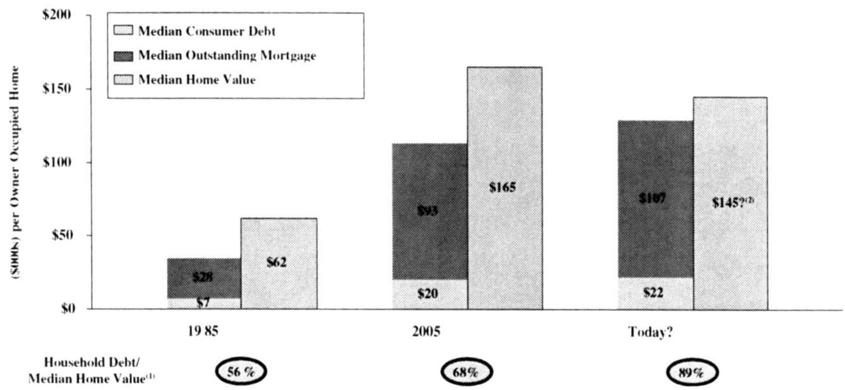

Fig. 4.8 Household debt/home values (1985, 2005, 2008).
Source: U.S. Census Bureau, Federal Reserve Flow of Funds, S&P Case-Shiller Index.

the peak is reached in 2006 at a value of 0.3 but thereafter the ratio declines sharply. Thus, prior to outbreak of the crisis in Summer of 2007, there was certainly credible adverse evidence about the value of the underlying housing assets (see also Figure 3.11 on the time-series of ABX indices).

What made the housing price shock primarily a solvency issue was the high leverage in both the household sector and the financial sector. Figure 4.8 graphs estimates of household debt over home values of the median household. The median value of outstanding mortgage principal amount of owner-occupied units and the consumer credit per household was derived from the U.S. Census Bureau and Federal Reserve Flow of Funds, and the 2008 median home value was adjusted from the 2005 fourth quarter value using the Case-Shiller National Home Price Index. The ratio of household debt to home values stood at a remarkable 89% in 2008 compared to just 68% in 2005, and 56% twenty years earlier, in 1985. Similarly, Table 3.1 showed that the financial sector was likewise significantly exposed to housing values.

So right from its inception, the financial crisis of 2007–2009 appears to have been a crisis of solvency not just for the household sector but also for the financial sector. It is indeed the case that when a large number of economic agents de-lever at once, market prices will reflect liquidity discounts (Allen and Gale, 2007) and short-term creditors will "run" as debt capacity of assets deteriorates due to the market-driven discounts (Acharya et al., 2008). Nevertheless, the primary cause of both of these problems is the need to de-lever and the fact that the leveraged agents are all on the same side of the trade. We therefore believe that the "liquidity problems" witnessed in this crisis, while clearly a symptom of some market segmentation and mark-to-market treatment in regulatory capital buffers of banks, they ultimately were connected to at least some solvency problems.

The root cause of the crisis as a solvency problem of households and the financial sector is perhaps one explanation for why the highly innovative liquidity injection facilities created by the Federal Reserve (and other Central Banks) in its lender-of-last-resort function did not ultimately succeed in stemming the crisis. Between Fall 2007 and December 2008, the Federal Reserve effectively created backstop facilities for most kinds of assets that experienced stress in the crisis; it provided longer-term lending facilities against the highest-quality collateral, extended discount window to securities firms and investment banks, lent against high-quality illiquid asset-backed securities, lent for purchases of ABCP and unsecured CP, provided liquidity to money market funds, and purchased assets of the GSE's. These were liquidity-targeted measures, and were unlikely to save the day if the underlying problem was insolvency. Indeed, any balance-sheet restructuring or solvency stress tests occurred only after fourteen months into the crisis, following the failure of Lehman Brothers in mid-September 2008. At that stage the crisis had already taken fully systemic proportions.

In fact, some of the markets the central banks attempted to restore through liquidity injections — such as illiquid mortgage-backed securities — continue to remain moribund over two years after the onset of the crisis due to the substantial overhang of debt and poor quality assets on the financial sector's balance sheets. As an illustration of this point, consider Figure 3.11 again which shows the price behavior of ABX of AAA-rated subprime tranches issued in the first and second halves of 2006 and 2007. The plot shows that in spite of the significant economic and financial stimulus, and government backing to support leveraged purchases of these assets, the tranches have recovered little as of February 2010, especially the tranches based on 2007 assets. From their lows of 20–30 cents on a dollar, these tranches have only recovered about 10 cents, highlighting that even fifteen months after bank recapitalizations these assets' prices remain depressed relative to par. This is strongly suggestive of poor cash flow realizations and quality of underlying mortgages rather than of a persistent liquidity discount.

Some of the worst assets, originated in 2006 and 2007, were taken over by regulators (explicitly or through government back-stops) while rescuing Bear Stearns and Citigroup, and are generating losses even to date on the regulators' books. Financial Times, February 16 2010 ("Bear property losses weigh on Fed") reports that the U.S. Federal Reserve is sitting on significant paper losses on the real estate assets in its Maiden Lane I portfolio acquired in the Bear Stearns rescue in March 2008, with much of the red ink coming from debt used to back some of the most high-profile buyout deals of the bubble years (e.g., Hilton Hotels which is being restructured and Extended Stay which is in bankruptcy). The assets — all of which came from Bear's mortgage desk — were originally valued at \$30bln and at the end of 2009, they were said to be worth \$27.1bln, about 10% loss, in spite of the economic stimulus and recovery. Commercial real estate holdings fell from \$7.7bln valuation to \$4bln. "It was the scrapings off the slaughterhouse floor. It started with the things that were not good enough to get securitized". While the Fed Chairman Ben Bernanke insists that they will ultimately not make losses on these portfolios, the temporary valuations of these assets have not yet rebounded, suggesting that the worst assets might be sitting in regulatory balance sheets, masking the true profitability of the banking sector portfolio from pre-Lehman days.

5

Conclusion

We have argued in this essay that there was a fundamental shift in the business model of large, complex financial institutions during the period of 2003–2Q 2007. This new business model led to their "manufacturing" tail risks that were systemic in nature. This involved, inter alia, selling deep out-of-the-money guarantees to off-balance sheet vehicles and holding little capital against them, or warehousing AAA-rated tranches of subprime mortgage-backed assets and financing their purchase with deposits and short-term commercial paper. They did this without sufficient capital to back the associated market, credit, and liquidity risk exposures. We conclude that the propensity of LCFIs to take on these risk exposures reflected an overriding risk-shifting incentive. The specific forms of this involved the use of complex innovations to arbitrage regulatory capital requirements.

While conclusive empirical evidence explaining the cause of such a shift in the banking model is worth pursuing, the history of bank regulation and the dynamics of the financial intermediation business itself suggest that there are several contributing factors. These include (a) increased competition which has eroded the profit margins in the traditional banking model and thus the "franchise value" of banks,

(b) explicit or implicit provision of government guarantees without appropriate charges or fees for the insurance cover implied and without ring-fencing of guarantees for the originally intended purposes, and (c) a passive regulatory stance toward the arbitrage of capital requirements on the part of the financial intermediaries themselves. The erosion of franchise values made it attractive for LCFIs to increase leverage. Mispriced government guarantees and lack of ring-fencing meant that tail risks could be manufactured without affecting the cost of funding. The lax enforcement of capital requirements allowed these tail risks to be retained on- or off-their balance sheets. Macroeconomic factors such as low interest rates in the United States and large capital flows into trade-deficit countries such as the United States and the United Kingdom undoubtedly amplified the inherent propensity for seeking tail-risk in the financial sector.

Our recommendations in Acharya et al. (2010a,b) for reforming financial sector regulation directly address some of these underlying drivers. Below we provide a brief summary of our proposals:

First, systemic financial intermediaries like LCFIs must be charged fees (effectively insurance premiums) commensurate with the explicit or implicit government insurance they enjoy on a continuous basis, and not just when resolution funds have been depleted in crisis situations. These insurance premiums would be explicitly linked to their overall risk profiles and insured deposit base — as well as to their total leverage given the likelihood of ex-post forbearance when large players fail.

Second, there should be an additional fee or premium that is tied specifically to the systemic risk of banks and other LCFIs given the reality that systemic failures are associated not just with ex-post forbearance but also with significant negative externalities bearing on the rest of the financial sector and the real economy. While systemic risk is difficult to quantify, a start needs to be made in this direction.

Third, it must be recognized that charging of such fees or insurance premiums depends inherently on the regulatory assessment of risk. Even with market-based data and good supervisory intelligence, macro-prudential risk assessment might well be imperfect, since there are always internal issues related to capital and risk allocations whose consequences are not fully reflected or visible, even at the level of their own boards and much less to outside stakeholders. To this end, some discipline that is based on realized outcomes is necessary. This might be some type of "contingent capital" that could for example take the form of debt that automatically converts into equity when bad firm-level or systemic states materialize. There are plenty of alternatives of this nature that could be helpful.

Finally, it is worth considering — whether by regulatory fiat or through appropriate capital charges — if a form of functional separation or carve-outs needs to be enforced, as is being advocated, by Paul Volcker, Mervyn King, and others who are deeply skeptical about the efficacy of finely tuned regulation of financial firms that have time and again proven their skill at regulatory avoidance and arbitrage. This separation would carve out the traditional banking and intermediation activities of lending and underwriting from the more risk-prone activity of proprietary trading or effectively running an in-house hedge fund, which are the likely "manufacturing" centers for tail risk and systemic instability. Enforcing or inducing a separation of this type might well erode some economies of scope between hedging and trading activities at banks and other LCFIs. In return, it could render more tractable the immense moral hazard problem arising from accordance of government guarantees and the inevitable opacity and complexity associated with financial innovations aimed at exploiting loopholes and undermining systemic safety and soundness. Functional separation may well be a small price to pay for enhanced robustness of the financial system.

A

Appendix: Tail Risk in the Rest of the World

Over the years there has been a great deal of debate about the relative properties of alternative financial systems around the world: How do they differ from one another, and how do they compare in achieving what financial systems are supposed to achieve in terms of the public interest — an optimum combination of efficiency, innovation, and global competitiveness, balanced against stability and robustness? Financial systems do indeed differ widely among national financial systems in terms of the role of universal banks and financial conglomerates, specialized financial intermediaries of various kinds, government-owned and hybrid financial services providers, financial cooperatives, and the like. The financial crisis of 2007–2009 provides an unusual opportunity to perform a robustness check into the resilience of financial systems in terms of their inherent fragility, propagation of financial shocks, and their transmission to the real sector of the economies.

The available date on write-downs of impaired assets that are at the center of the crisis suggest that non-U.S. financial intermediaries were as involved as their U.S. competitors in taking losses (Exhibit 1). By the end of 2006 and the onset of the crisis, a small number of non-US banks had pushed into the upper brackets of the fixed-income origination

Exhibit 1. Exposure Write-Downs and Capital Raised (in billion dollars) as of October 2009.

Firm	Loss	Capital
Wachovia Corporation	101.9	11
Citigroup Inc.	88.3	109.3
Merrill Lynch & Co	55.9	29.9
UBS AG	50.6	32.9
Washington Mutual Inc.	45.3	12.1
Bank of America Corp.	42.7	78.5
HSBC Holdings Plc	42.2	23.5
JPMorgan Chase & Co	33.3	44.7
HBOS Plc	25.7	22.4
National City Corp.	25.2	8.9
Wells Fargo & Company	23.4	41.8
Morgan Stanley	21.5	24.6
Royal Bank of Scotland	20.7	48.5
Deutsche Bank AG	16.4	5.9
Lehman Brothers Holdings	16.2	13.9
Bayerische Landesbank	16.1	20
Credit Suisse Group AG	15.8	11.9
Barclays Plc	14.2	26.8
ING Groep N.V.	14	19.4
IKB Deutsche Industries	13.9	11.4
Societe Generale	8.9	11.1
Fortis	8.9	21.7
Credit Agricole S.A.	7.7	12
Natixis	7.7	7.8
BNP Paribas	7.6	3.4
Mizuho Financial Group	7.5	8.2
Canadian Imperial Bank	7.3	2.5
PNC Financial Service	7.2	8.1
Goldman Sachs Group	7.1	20.5
DZ Bank AG	7	0
Dexia SA	6.2	8.6
KBC Groep NV	6.2	7.4
SunTrust Banks Inc	6.1	4.9
UniCredit SpA	6	10.1
Bank of China Ltd	5.9	0
Other Asian Banks	5.5	16.9
Other European Banks	5.5	4.5
Hypo Real Estate Holdings	5.4	0
Indymac Bancorp	5.2	0

Source: Bloomberg

league tables — notably Deutsche Bank AG, UBS AG, and Credit Suisse. As the volume of fixed-income originations shifted to asset-backed securities (ABS) and mortgage-backed securities (MBS) as well as collateralized debt obligations (CDOs) and related instruments, one would expect these firms to have also taken on "pipeline" exposures to these instruments comparable to American firms like Merrill Lynch and Citigroup. The incentive for these non-U.S. wholesale intermediaries — all of whom are universal banks or financial conglomerates — to invest in these securities and assume warehouse risk exposures would have been the same as for the U.S. firms. In fact, in some cases such as UBS the incentive could have been even greater due to the abnormally low cost of funds attributable to the large private banking divisions. Consequently, as confirmed by Exhibit 1, in the losses taken by the big wholesale financial intermediaries as of late-2009 the major European players featured no less than their American rivals.

Beyond the key originators and intermediaries were the banks that engaged minimally in the intermediation process but principally took on the role of investors in what ultimately became damaged assets. Again, Exhibit 1 shows that over half of the top fifty losers were

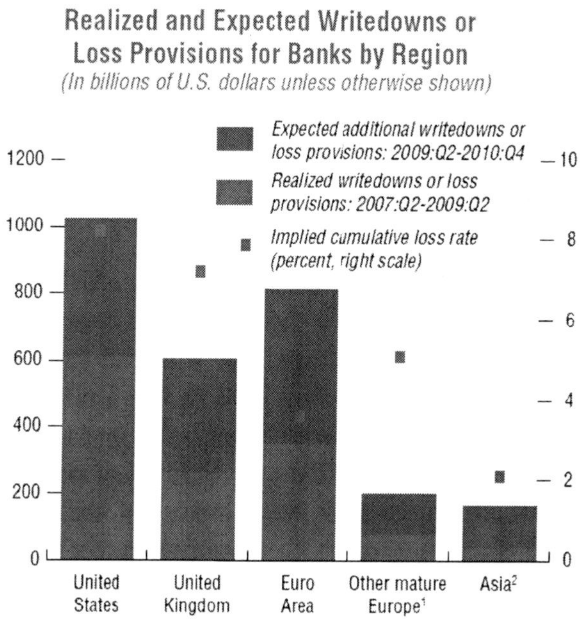

Exhibit 2

Source: IMF staff estimates.

[1]Includes Denmark, Iceland, Norway, Sweden, and Switzerland.

[2]Includes Australia, Hong Kong SAR, Japan, New Zealand, and Singapore.

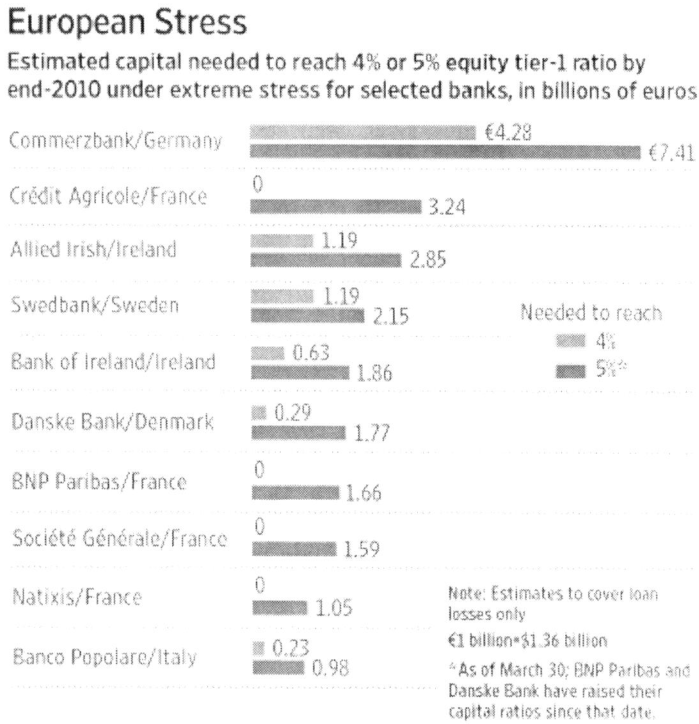

Exhibit 3
(*Source*: International Monetary Fund, Global Financial Stability Report, April 2009)
Keefe, Bruyette & Woods

non-U.S. banks. A number of these (most notably, ABN AMRO, HBOS, and IKB) had set up off-balance sheet vehicles (conduits and SIVs) to avoid the capital requirements associated with this exposure. Northern Rock that collapsed in September 2008 in the United Kingdom was also heavily reliant on wholesale asset-backed paper and had grown its mortgage book multifold with little growth in retail deposit base. When the crisis hit, these banks took large losses (in some cases arguably larger than indicated due to less conservative marks as to their value) and could not roll over their leverage as they had arranged little capital buffer to guard against the underlying credit and rollover risks. Exhibit 2 shows the IMF's estimates of the magnitude of those losses realized as of 2009 (Q2) and the expected write-downs through the end of 2010, showing European losses to be far higher than American losses.

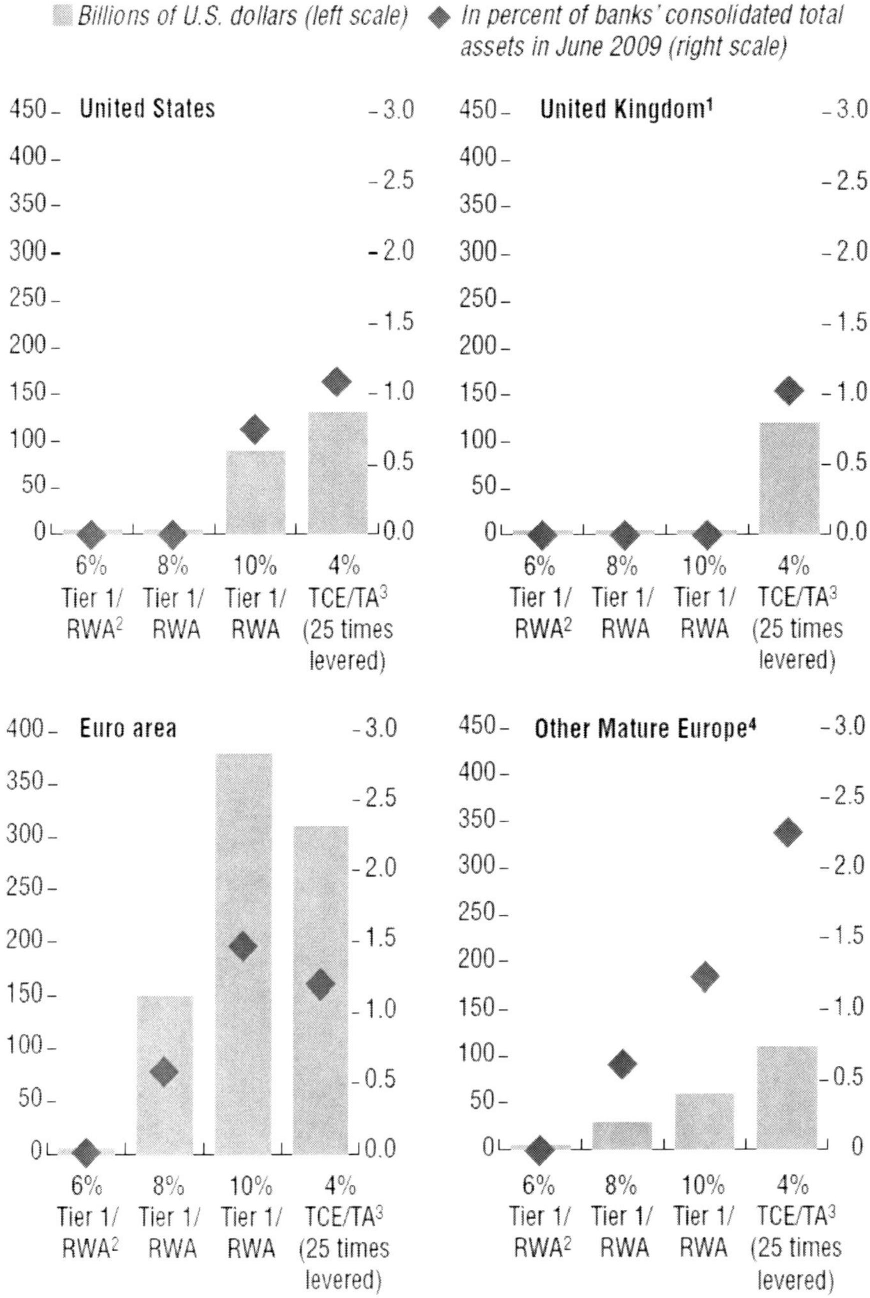

Exhibit 4 Estimates additional capital raising needed to reach specific targets.
Source: IMF staff estimates.

The losses booked so far and the apparent difference in marked asset valuations between the United States and Europe suggests further pain for the surviving institutions. Exhibit 3 estimates the additional capital that would have to be raised by individual European banks to reach 4% and 5%, respectively, of risk-weighted assets under the Basle 2 standards. This assessment is broadened in Exhibit 4 to banks home-based in specific European countries, according to IMF estimates in October 2009. It is clear from this last exhibit that if the U.S. marks prove to be more accurate than the continental European marks, then the European banks will have a great deal of capital raising to do given the significant tail risk of real estate and the global economy at large to which they built exposures leading up to the crisis.

References

Acharya, V. V., T. Cooley, M. Richardson, and I. Walter (2010a), 'Market failures and regulatory failures: Lessons from past and present crises'. In: M. Kawai and E. Prasad (eds.): *forthcoming Financial Sector Regulation and Reforms in Emerging Markets*. Washington, DC: Brookings Institution Press.

Acharya, V. V., T. Cooley, M. Richardson, and I. Walter (2010b), *Regulating Wall Street: The New Architecture of Global Finance*. forthcoming, New York University Stern School of Business and John Wile & Sons.

Acharya, V. V., D. Gale, and T. Yorulmazer (2008), 'Rollover risk and market freezes'. Working Paper, New York University Stern School of Business.

Acharya, V. V., M. Pagano, and P. Volpin (2009a), 'Seeking alpha: Excess risk taking and competition for managerial talent'. Working Paper, New York University Stern School of Business.

Acharya, V. V. and M. Richardson (2009a), 'Causes of the financial crisis'. *Critical Review* **21**(2–3), 195–210.

Acharya, V. V. and M. Richardson (2009b), *Restoring Financial Stability: How to Repair a Failed System*. New York University Stern School of Business and John Wiley & Sons.

Acharya, V. V., J. Santos, and T. Yorulmazer (2009b), 'Systemic risk and deposit insurance premiums'. *forthcoming, Economic Policy Review, Federal Reserve Bank of New York.*

Acharya, V. V. and P. Schnabl (2009), 'Do global banks spread global imbalances? The case of asset-backed commercial paper during the financial crisis of 2007–2009'. Working Paper, New York University Stern School of Business.

Acharya, V. V., P. Schnabl, and G. Suarez (2009c), 'Securitization without risk transfer'. Working Paper, New York University Stern School of Business.

Acharya, V. V. and P. Volpin (2010), 'Corporate governance externalities'. *Review of Finance* **14**(1), 1–33.

Adrian, T. and H. S. Shin (2009), 'The shadow banking system: Implications for financial regulation'. FRB of New York Staff Report No. 382.

Akerlof, G. and R. Shiller (2009), *Animal Spirits: How Human Psychology Drives the Economy, and Why It Matters for Global Capitalism.* Princeton University Press.

Allen, F. and D. Gale (2000), 'Bubbles and Crises'. *Economic Journal* **110**, 236–255.

Allen, F. and D. Gale (2007), *Understanding Financial Crises.* Clarendon Lectures in Finance, Oxford University Press.

Ashcraft, A. and T. Schuermann (2008), 'Understanding the Securitization of Subprime Mortgage Credit'. Federal Reserve Bank of New York Working Paper.

Bernanke, B. S. (2000), *Essays on the Great Depression.* Princeton University Press.

Bernanke, B. S. (2005), 'The global saving glut and the U.S. current account deficit'. Speech delivered for the Sandridge Lecture at the Virginia Association of Economists, Richmond, March 10, www.federalreserve.gov/boarddocs/speeches/2005/200503102/default.htm.

Berndt, A. and A. Gupta (2008), 'Moral hazard and adverse selection in the originate-to-distribute model of bank credit'. Working Paper, Carnegie Mellon University.

Bruner, R. and S. D. Carr (2007), *The Panic of 1907: Lessons Learned from the Market's Perfect Storm.* John Wiley and Sons.

Caballero, R. J., E. Farhi, and P. O. Gourinchas (2008), 'An Equilibrium Model of Global Imbalances and Low Interest Rates'. *American Economic Review* **98**(1), 358–393.

Caballero, R. J. and A. Krishnamurthy (2009), 'Global Imbalances and Financial Fragility'. *American Economic Review Papers and Proceedings* **99**(2), 584–588.

Calomiris, C. and C. Kahn (1991), 'The role of demandable debt in structuring optimal banking arrangements'. *American Economic Review* **81**(3), 497–513.

Cordell, L. R., G. D. Mac Donald, and M. E. Wohar (1993), 'Corporate ownership and the thrift crisis'. *Journal of Law and Economics* **36**(2), 719–756.

Dell'Ariccia, G., D. Igan, and L. Laeven (2008), 'Credit booms and lending standards: Evidence from the subprime mortgage market'. Working Paper, International Monetary Fund.

Diamond, D. W. (1984), 'Financial intermediation and delegated monitoring'. *The Review of Economic Studies* **51**(3), 393–414.

Diamond, D. W. and R. G. Rajan (2001), 'Liquidity risk, liquidity creation and financial fragility: A theory of banking'. *Journal of Political Economy* **109**(2), 287–327.

Engle, R. F. (2009), 'Long run skewness and systemic risk'. In: *Presentation at International Association of Financial Engineers (IAFE).* Mimeo, New York University Stern School of Business.

Ennis, H. and H. S. Malek (2005), 'Bank risk of failure and the too-big-to-fail policy'. *Federal Reserve Bank of Richmond Economic Quarterly* **91**, 21–44.

Federal Deposit Insurance Corporation (1997), 'History of the eighties — Lessons for the future: Volume I: An examination of the banking crises of the 1980s and early 1990s'. (online at www.fdic.gov/bank/historical/history/vol1.html).

Friedman, M. and A. J. Schwartz (1971), *A Monetary History of The United States 1867–1960.* Princeton University Press.

Gabaix, X. and A. Landier (2008), 'Why has CEO pay increased so much?'. *Quarterly Journal of Economics* **123**, 49–100.

Gorton, G. (1985), 'Clearing houses and the origin of Central Banking in the United States'. *Journal of Economic History* **XLV**(2), 277–283.

Gorton, G. (2008), 'The Panic of 2007'. Yale University working paper.

Gorton, G. (2009), 'Slapped in the face by the invisible hand: Banking and the panic of 2007'. Working Paper, Yale University.

Gorton, G. and G. Pennacchi (1990), 'Financial intermediaries and liquidity creation'. *Journal of Finance* **45**(1), 49–71.

Hovakimian, A. and E. J. Kane (2000), 'Effectiveness of capital regulation at U.S. commercial banks, 1985 to 1994'. *The Journal of Finance* **55**(1), 451–468.

Jensen, M. C. and W. H. Meckling (1976), 'Theory of the firm: Managerial behavior, agency costs and ownership structure'. *Journal of Financial Economics* **3**(4), 305–360.

John, K. and T. A. John (1993), 'Top-management compensation and capital structure'. *Journal of Finance* **48**, 949–974.

Keeley, M. C. (1990), 'Deposit insurance, risk, and market power in banking'. *the American Economic Review* **80**(5), 1183–1200.

Keys, B., T. Mukherjee, A. Seru, and V. Vig (2008), 'Did securitization lead to lax screening? Evidence form subprime loans?'. Working Paper, London Business School.

Krishnamurthy, A. (2008), 'The financial meltdown: Data and diagnoses'. Northwestern University working paper.

Kroszner, R. (2000), 'Lessons from financial crises: The role of clearinghouses'. *Journal of Financial Services Research*, Springer **18**(2), 157–171.

Kroszner, R. and W. Melick (2009), 'The response of the federal reserve to the banking and financial crisis of 2007/2008'. working paper.

Kroszner, R. S. and P. E. Strahan (1996), 'Regulatory incentives and the thrift crisis: Dividends, mutual-to-stock conversions, and financial distress'. *the Journal of Finance* **51**(4), 1285–1319.

Kroszner, R. S. and P. E. Strahan (2007), 'Regulation and Deregulation of the I.S. Banking Industry: Causes, Consequences and Implications for the Future'. In: N. Rose (ed.): *Economic Regulation and its Reform: What have we Learned?* University of Chicago Press.

Lucas, D. and R. L. McDonald (2006), 'An options-based approach to evaluating the risk of Fannie Mae and Freddie Mac'. *Journal of Monetary Economics* **53**(1), 155–176.

Marcus, A. and I. Shaked (1984), 'The valuation of FDIC deposit insurance using option pricing estimates'. *Journal of Money, Credit and Banking* **16**, 444–460.

Meltzer, A. (2004), 'Monetarism revisited'. *World Economics Journal* **5**(2), 161–164.

Mian, A. and A. Sufi (2008), 'The consequences of mortgage credit expansion: Evidence from the 2007 mortgage default crisis'. *Quarterly Journal of Economics*, forthcoming.

Morgan, D. and K. Stiroh (2005), 'Too big to fail after all these years'. Federal Reserve Bank of New York staff report.

Myers, S. C. (1977), 'Determinants of corporate borrowing'. *Journal of Financial Economics* **5**(2), 147–175.

Myers, S. C. and N. S. Majluf (1984), 'Corporate financing and investment decisions when firms have information that investors do not have'. *Journal of Financial Economics* **13**(2), 187–221.

Obstfeld, M. and K. Rogoff (2009), 'Global imbalances and the financial crisis: Products of common causes'. Working Paper, Harvard University.

O'Hara, M. and W. Shaw (1990), 'Deposit insurance and wealth effects: The value of being too big to fail'. *Journal of Finance* **45**, 1587–1601.

Passmore, W. (2005), 'The GSE Implicit Subsidy and the value of Government Ambiguity'. *Real Estate Economics* **33**(3), 465–486.

Penas, M. and H. Unal (2004), 'Gains in bank mergers: Evidence from the bond markets'. *Journal of Financial Economics* **74**, 149–179.

Pennacchi, G. (1987), 'A reexamination of the over- (or under-) pricing of deposit insurance'. *Journal of Money, Credit and Banking* **19**, 340–360.

Pinto, E. (2008), 'Statement before the committee on oversight and government reform'. US House of Representatives, December 9.

Portes, R. (2009), 'Global imbalances'. In: M. Dewatripont, X. Freixas, and R. Portes (eds.): *Macroeconomic stability and financial regulation*. CEPR, pp. 9–26.

Rajan, R. (2008), 'Bankers' pay is deeply flawed'. Financial Times, January 9.

Reinhart, C. and K. Rogoff (2008), 'This time is different: A panoramic view of eight centuries of financial crises'. NBER working paper.

Saunders, A., E. Strock, and N. G. Travlos (1990), 'Ownership structure, deregulation, and bank risk taking'. *the Journal of Finance* **45**(2), 643–654.

Shin, H. S. (2009), 'Securitization and financial stability'. Paper presented as the Economic Journal Lecture at the Royal Economic Society meeting, Warwick, March 2008.

Stern, G. and R. Feldman (2004), *Too Big to Fail: The Hazards of Bank Bailouts*. Washington D.C: Brookings Institution Press.

Stiglitz, J. (1992), 'Banks versus markets as mechanisms for allocating and coordinating investment'. In: J. Roumasset and S. Barr (eds.): *The Economics of Cooperation*. Boulder: Westview Press, Inc.

Stiroh, K. (2002), 'Diversification in banking? Is noninterest income the answer?'. Working Paper, Federal Reserve Bank of New York.

Stock, J. H. and M. W. Watson (2002), 'Has the business cycle changed and why?'. *NBER Macroeconomics Annual* pp. 159–218.

Taylor, J. (2009), 'The financial crisis and the policy responses: An empirical analysis of what went wrong'. Working Paper, Stanford University.

White, L. J. (1991), *The S&L Debacle: Public Policy Lessons for Bank and Thrift Regulation*. Oxford University Press.

White, L. J. (2006), 'Good intentions gone awry: A policy analysis of the SEC's regulation of the bond rating industry'. Policy Brief #2006-PB-05, Networks Financial Institute, Indiana State University.

Lightning Source UK Ltd.
Milton Keynes UK
174419UK00001B/1/P

9 781601 983404